A Taste for Salt Water

By R. Laforest Perkins

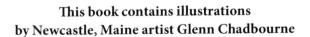

This book contains illustrations
by Newcastle, Maine artist Glenn Chadbourne

A Taste for Salt Water (First Printing)
©2012 R. Laforest Perkins
Second printing, 2014, revised. Third printing, 2016 revised.
ISBN 978-1-936447-07-7

All rights reserved. No part of this book may be reproduced in any form or by any electronic or mechanical means, including information storage and retrieval systems, without permission in writing from the author, except by a reviewer, who may quote brief passages in review.

Since retiring from the YMCA in 2000, I was looking for something to do with my time, and I decided to try to write true stories about some of the oceanic adventures I experienced at different times in my life.

I did not begin recording these stories until I was in my mid to late seventies, so I had to think long and hard to recall what I could remember. It has been impossible to remember every detail of these stories, and in what order they happened, but I have done the best that I could without embellishment.

I have tried to recount how my two brothers, Phil and Bernie, fit in. Phil was two years younger, and Bernie was three years younger, than I.

There is much about what I have written that has left me with a yearning for the "good old days".

R. Laforest Perkins
Waldoboro, Maine
April 6, 2007

CONTENTS

BOSTON TO ROCKLAND ON THE STEAMER BELFAST..........3

DESTINATION: NORTH HAVEN..........9

THE YACHT *SARAH B.* COMES TO LYNN..........24

THE FISHING TRIPS..........31

THE GRAVES LEDGE LIGHTHOUSE TRIP..........33

THE GLOUCESTER TRIPS..........37

THE HAPPY HOME BAKERS' EXCURSION..........44

THE REGATTA..........47

THE TOW JOB..........50

THE SINKING..........51

THE PROVINCETOWN TRIPS..........54

DISASTER: THE DROWNING..........55

THE ALTERATIONS..........56

SHORT, SHORT STORIES..........58

SALT WATER CAMPING..........63

TROOP SHIP EXPERIENCES..........64

THE HERMIT OF PLUM ISLAND..........68

THE HERMIT OF GRAPE ISLAND..........70

THE COPPER SPIKE..........72

ELMER BOYD, MARINE MECHANIC..........74

THE YACHT *EARLY TIMES*..........78

THE AUTHOR..........81

BOSTON TO ROCKLAND ON THE STEAMER *BELFAST*

Back around 1933 my mother announced to me and my two younger brothers that we were going to take a trip to Maine on a steamboat to visit Grampy Dyer and other relatives. I was about six years old then, my brothers were about four and three, and this was all new to us.

When the day came to go, we piled our luggage into our 1928 Cadillac Club Coupe, and my father drove us from our house in Lynn to Boston.

When we arrived at the dock in the late afternoon, we stood looking at the big white ship tied up port side to the dock. My father handled the luggage, placing it in the loading area. I stared at the ship's name, *Belfast*, which was carved into about a six-foot quarterboard in gold lettering on a black background.

Two or three stevedores were loading luggage and freight on two-wheeled hand trucks and running them down the ramp with luggage higher than the handles into the ship's forecastle. After dropping their loads, they ran back up the ramp. Once in a while, the men would take large handkerchiefs out of their back pockets to wipe the sweat off their heads. There were no fork trucks on the docks in those days.

When the freight was aboard, the passengers were allowed down the ramp to the forecastle. A company employee was sitting at a card table, and checked our names against a passenger registration list. Then, he reached down, scooped up a handful of keys from a bucket, looked at the numbers on them, and selected the one that would unlock our stateroom. A matron in a clean starched uniform appeared. She took the key and led us along the deck. We went up a wide stairway and down a long central carpeted corridor to our room.

The ship had a steel hull, and its superstructure was of wood construction. Everything was painted gleaming white, inside and out. I noticed the ship's two stacks came up through the decks along the centerline, and took up a lot of space. Inside the ship, they were encased in matched wood strips, and also painted white. The deck we were quartered on had a double row of staterooms on each side. The outside staterooms had a door opening to the weather deck and a window. The inside rooms had a door opening to the central corridor, and were ventilated through a ceiling duct. I suspect the rate might have been cheaper for an inside room.

The matron unlocked our stateroom door and showed us in. She opened the small wooden door to the ventilator shaft, and left us to return with a large ceramic pitcher of water.

The rooms were probably not much larger than six feet by six feet. There were two neatly made up bunks, one over the other, on the back wall. A small wardrobe closet was to the right. To the left, was a small cabinet with a big ceramic wash basin where the matron left the water pitcher. There were no water pipes, faucets, or drains. A space underneath held a chamber pot.

After the matron had left, my mother gave us egg salad sandwiches and something to drink, a lunch she had prepared at home.

Toward evening, we sensed a light vibration, the ship's whistle sounded a long blast, and we left the dock. We begged our mother to let us go out on deck to look at the passing scenery, but she refused, saying she thought we might fall overboard.

It was close to bedtime for us then, and, having nothing else to do anyway, my mother took my youngest brother into the upper bunk with her, and told my other brother and me to get into the lower.

I don't know how long it took us to get to sleep, but I awakened sometime in the night to find the ship steaming steadily, without labor, and taking a moderate roll. I jumped out of the bunk and stood on the deck for some time, enjoying the sway of the ship, and listening to the creaking of the superstructure. When I tired of that, I got back in bed and was soon fast asleep.

The next thing I heard was my mother telling us we had to get up and get dressed in a hurry, because we were soon to dock at Rockland.

It was daylight as we left our stateroom and got to the weather deck at the disembarking station. The ship had stopped at the wharf. A deckhand tossed a light throw line to a dock worker, but missed his target, and the line fell into the water. He quickly retrieved it, and the dock man caught it on the next toss, hauling up the ship's heavier dock line to make the ship fast.

When we left the ship, it was still early in the morning under cold and foggy skies. Walking up the ramp, the sea water looked cold and dark, and our nostrils filled with the odors of marine life, sea vegetation,

A Taste for Salt Water

The Belfast joined the Eastern Steamship Company fleet on the Boston to Bangor run in 1909 and continued until 1935. Faster and more reliable than her predecessors, she and her 1907 sister ship, the Camden, are the most remembered of the "Boston Boats." (Photo submitted courtesy Rockland Maine Historical Society)

and wet pilings. We waited at the terminal for the steamer that would take us to our final destination, the island of North Haven.

A nice model of the *Belfast*, about three-feet long, is displayed in a glass case at the Maine Maritime Museum at Bath, just down the street from where the ship was built. One of its quarterboards is mounted at the top of the display case. There is a fifty-fifty chance it was the one I saw mounted on the port side over seventy years ago.

A sign in the case reads: —*Belfast,* Built by Bath Iron Works in 1909, the *City of Belfast* ran for many years between Boston and Penobscot Bay in the service of the Eastern Steamship Corporation. On 27 December 1935, this vessel made the last steamer run from Maine to Boston. It was sold in 1935, renamed *Arrow,* and re-commissioned for New York to Providence service.

The *Belfast* was 320-feet long, and had a 40-foot beam. It was powered by steam turbines, and driven by triple screws.

The steamer Belfast, owned by the Eastern Steamship Line, steams downstream [sic] past Odom Ledge off Sandy Point circa 1910. Bangor Daily News, January 1 1999

The circa 1910 card depicts the steamer Belfast approaching its dock in Belfast. During the early 20th century, steamers connected Maine ports with Boston and the outside world. Bangor Daily News, January 1 1999

The steamer North Haven was one of the ferries for local island transport that used Tillson's Wharf in the 1930s. By the 1950s passenger steamers were replaced by modern automobile-carrying ferry boats. (Photo submitted courtesy Rockland Maine Historical Society)

DESTINATION: NORTH HAVEN

After purchasing our ferry tickets in the office on the Tillson Street wharf, our luggage was loaded on the steamer *North Haven,* which had just arrived from an island trip. We went aboard, and found the cabin very roomy. It contained several rows of benches for the passengers. The sky was overcast and after casting off, we sailed through light, patchy fog all the way over to the island. We passed the Rockland breakwater lighthouse, then the half way gong buoy, and veered to port after passing the Fiddler's Ledge marker, toward the North Haven pier. On approach, the tide was quite low, and we breathed in a strong odor of rockweed and mud flats, and felt a little cold from the damp air. Just before we got to the pier, we passed a small power boat containing two men seated in a small forward cabin, that bobbed up and down in the *North Haven*'s wake, and sounded a siren for a few seconds—the only time I ever heard one on a pleasure boat, and it sounded for no particular reason.

After the *North Haven* was tied up to the pier, we walked up the gangway into the freight shed, and out to the parking lot. My uncle, Thorne Dyer, was there with his Model A Ford roadster, waiting to pick us up. He somehow got our baggage and two of us boys into the rumble seat compartment. Everyone else rode on the front seat.

The ride to Grandfather Avery Dyer's house only took a few minutes, and we found ourselves going along dirt roads, smelling a grassy odor from the fields, and the scent given off by the spruce trees that were growing there in abundance. This was very different from the paved streets and concrete sidewalks we were accustomed to in the more heavily populated Lynn, and we found it not a bit unpleasant.

We turned left when we got to my grandfather's road, which was across from the fresh water pond near the middle of the island.

His home was a few hundred feet from the main road.

There were three small single-story buildings on Avery's property, lined up in a row. The one nearest the road was a bunkhouse, maybe about 16 feet square, and contained seven or eight metal cots meant for sleeping one person each.

The next building was a small tool shed and workshop, maybe about

8 or 10 feet square. A large slab of dried salt cod hung in a corner.

The third building was my grandfather's house, which had two rooms, a kitchen and a bedroom. The bedroom was walled with something like sheetrock paneling. The kitchen was not finished.

A cast iron wood stove was used for heating the house and cooking food, and it had a tank on the end of it to heat spring water that was dumped into it from pails. The smoke pipe hung near the ceiling, and ran to the back wall, where it was connected to a ceramic pipe chimney fastened to the back of the house. An iron sink was mounted on the back wall under the smoke pipe, and pails of spring water were left near it for washing and drinking purposes. Waste water was piped outside, onto the ground. There were kerosene lamps for lighting.

A large canvas wall tent was mounted on a wooden platform just beyond the house, and Uncle Thorne slept in it. A path between the house and the tent led to a two-hole outhouse in the woods, and the path continued farther beyond it into the woods to the spring.

An area near the road was used to store firewood in an uncovered pile, and the first time I went there, in 1933, an old 1920's-era touring car with no top on it was abandoned there between the road and the woodpile.

The driveway continued past Avery's property for a few hundred feet to Uncle Alfred and Aunt Edna Dyer's house, which was situated on a little knoll. Their two children were named Milton and Goldie.

A roomy building had been added to the back of Alfred's house for a workshop. He once built a small flat-bottomed boat there, which he called a punt. He showed us a pair of oars he had expertly made for it, using hand tools.

Alfred's barn housed two cows, a horse named Nellie, a pig, and, at one time, a sheep.

On the right hand side of the barn, Alfred built lobster boats. He had one under construction when we came, and I noticed he was planking it with wood strips that were about an inch-and-an-eighth square. Thorne told me it was called a "strip boat," explaining it was easier to plank a hull that way, but a little more challenging to repair because the strips were not only fastened to the ribs, but nailed to each other.

When we got to my grandfather's house on my first trip there, my aunt, Evelyn Dyer Goudie, was already there with her son, Bobbie, and daughter, Nancy. None of us had any reason to feel lonely there.

We often amused ourselves by wandering off to explore the area. I discovered a gravel excavation next door. An abutting pasture containing a lot of trees was close by, and I wandered through it, finding several animal skulls, and two dead seagulls.

Thorne fired a shotgun into the air occasionally, but I never knew what his target might have been. He shot a duck once which was made into a soup, but I didn't care for it.

My grandfather used to bake muffins in one of those pans having long, rounded bottoms. They were kind of tan color, and had a unique flavor all their own. Nobody knows how he made them. His recipe did not exist outside his head. In some of his quiet moments, he had a habit of taking a slab of sliced Edgeworth Pipe Tobacco out of a can, and rolling it in his hands to crumble it for the pipe he smoked every day.

I wandered over to a neighbor's barn one day, and picked up hay off of the floor to feed the cows. When I bent down to get another handful, a cow turned her head down sharply, causing her horn to strike me on the head, knocking me flat on the floor. Dazed and frightened, I decided not to try that again for a while.

We occasionally amused ourselves by jumping into the old touring car, and pretending we were driving it. We didn't stay in it very long, because rain water had soaked the exposed seating, and gave it a bad odor. We also liked to collect wood chips from the wood pile and bring them in to start the fire each morning. The fire was burning almost continuously during the day, keeping the kitchen uncomfortably hot.

My brother Phil did something to irk me in the kitchen one day, and when I went after him, he ducked into the bedroom, pulling the door closed after him. My little finger got shut in the jamb, and burst open. That hurt and bled a lot, and I cried a bit. The island doctor taped my finger back together.

I was walking around the tent one morning, and I decided to take a look under the platform. I spotted a pile of hen's eggs way under there, where no one could reach them. I thought that was a dumb place for a chicken to lay eggs. I decided to throw a couple of stones at them, which was difficult, because the area was so confined. I thought I might have hit one.

About mealtime, in the kitchen, I mentioned that I threw a few stones at some eggs under the tent. Immediately, my grandfather jumped up, bellowing that he had put them under there for a hen to sit on and hatch out. He was some mad! A few days later, the hen came walking by me, followed by about eighteen chicks. I bent down to pick one up and the hen flew at me in a rage, talons pointed right at me, and stirring up a lot of chaos from the wildly flapping wings. I knew enough not to try that again, after I stopped running.

My mother washed our faces and hands with a soapy cloth during the day. At one point, she decided my brothers and I needed a bath. A large, round galvanized iron tub was brought in, and laid on the kitchen floor. Warm water was bailed out of the stove tank, and dumped into it. Then the three of us were made to bathe in it, starting with Bernie, then Phil, and then me. By the time I got in, the water was cloudy, and unpleasant to bathe in. But I was told that water was scarce, so I did it, hoping I would not have that experience again.

There is a small fresh water pond at the southwestern corner of what was then Uncle Alfred's property, which was created when a dam was built across a small stream that flowed toward Pulpit Harbor. The top of the dam served as a driveway for a neighbor's house. Aunt Evelyn took a few of us kids for a walk to the pond one morning. Seeing a large tree that had fallen into the water, I got an impulse to run out onto it so I could look into the water, planning to stop near the end that was submerged. My feet started skidding down the moist, mossy growth that covered it, and I skidded right off the end in a big splash. I did not know how to swim, so I thrashed around, screaming in terror, trying to grasp the trunk, and inching my way to a spot where I could stand up and climb out, coughing and shaking all the while. My aunt just scowled at me, and gave me a scolding.

On our first stay at the island, we were discouraged to learn we had to pack up and go home. We loved island life. My father had come to the island with his Caddie the day before, to take us home.

We were waiting in the freight shed on the dock for a short while, before the steamer got there. All of a sudden, I heard a loud thud, and felt like I was in an earthquake. The floor shook under me, and the freight shed, built on piles, quivered and creaked in a scary manner for a few seconds. The steamer had apparently come in a little too fast. I felt startled and uneasy.

I once read that one time when the *North Haven* was coming up to the pier on schedule, the captain tried to signal the engineer to stop the ship by pulling on a rope attached to a bell in the engine room. But the rope snapped and went limp, startling a passenger who had been riding in the pilot house. The ship came to a stop at the right time, though, and the captain assured the passenger that the engineer was watching, and knew what to do.

In later years, around the beginning of World War II, the steam-powered ferries seemed to disappear. I remember going across at that time on a vessel built something like a dragger, maybe about fifty-feet long, and having a large, open rear cockpit for the passengers. I thought it was named the *Islander*, but I haven't found anyone who remembers it.

It was an overcast day, and the sea was rough enough to cause the ship to roll continuously. We were sitting on an aft seat in front of the transom, and behind a neatly stacked pile of red bricks for delivery offshore somewhere, when the rolling caused some of the bricks to topple off the pile, falling on the deck around our feet. The water calmed down as we entered the Thoroughfare, and we docked about ten minutes later.

Probably, at the time we wanted to return from that trip, Uncle Thorne said a power boat named the *J.O.* was available to take us to Rockland. It was foggy all the way over, but not too dense, and the sun shone through it from time to time. That boat was powerful and fast, the sea was calm, and we arrived in good time without incident.

When we got to the island once in that era, one of our relatives, Walker Ames, was driving a taxi, and he drove us to Uncle Alfred's house. We found Alfred with his hand bandaged. Milton had a blank cartridge pistol, and a shell got jammed in it. When Alfred tried to get it out, it discharged, injuring his hand, which made it difficult for him to do his farm work.

We got to see much of the work that went into running Alfred's farm. We watched them milk the cows, and they liked to squirt us with it when we were not expecting that to happen. Then they ran it through a separator, which extracted most of the heavy cream out of it. Aunt Edna asked me to crank the churn one day when she was making butter. Cooking and heating water was done on an iron wood stove.

It was a treat to eat Alfred's vegetables, fresh from his sizeable garden. We especially liked the fresh green peas, which did not compare to the canned ones we usually had back home.

In the evening, in kerosene lantern light, we sat around in the kitchen and told stories. There was no electricity, and, therefore, no radio. I remember my brother, Bernie, telling Alfred about some of the moving pictures we had seen, and explaining that big guys got into the theater for a quarter, and little guys got in for a dime, much to Alfred's amusement.

Alfred hitched up his horse to the hay wagon one evening, and took us for a hayride. Another evening, we went to a band concert on Main Street, on a raised lawn behind the water fountain. People clapped after each selection was played, and some of those who sat in their cars applauded by sounding their horns.

We got to watch Alfred cutting hay with his horse-drawn mower, and we helped shake it up with pitchforks a few days later to speed its drying. After that, we forked it into a wagon, which was then run into the barn. We forked it up into the loft, and kept pushing it back to compact it. I sneezed a lot on the dust. Some years after the horse had died, an old Chevrolet flatbed truck was used to tow the haying machinery.

Milton and I put the punt on the truck once, and drove to the fresh water pond across from their property to launch it. We fished with drop lines and worms. We did not get much fish, if any, that day, but I managed to hook a large eel. When I got it out of the water, I just held it up, hesitating to boat such an ugly looking creature. I was glad the line snapped, and the eel sank out of sight.

Milton had a .22 caliber rifle, and we shot at inanimate objects in the woods. We fired a couple of shots down a narrow salt waterway, to see the bullets skip along the surface. Population in that area was sparse, but we thought that might be risky business, so we did not do it again.

Someone boated Evelyn and my mother across the Thoroughfare with all five of us children to go blueberry picking at Vinalhaven. We stopped at Briggs Dyer's house for a visit. My mother gave us cans to put berries in, and I asked for a quart-sized one. After picking for a while in the blazing sun, with no water to drink, I soon lost interest, and wanted to quit. My mother said I had asked for the larger can, and could not go back until I filled it.

When we got back to Briggs' house, Phil went over to play with the family dog, which was tied to a rope. Phil had on short pants, and an unbuttoned shirt. We didn't know why, but the dog suddenly sunk his teeth into Phil's side, requiring first aid treatment. Then we walked back to the landing with our berries, and were boated back to North Haven. My mother canned the berries on the iron woodstove, and we brought them back to Lynn with us. We picked raspberries in isolated clearings in the woods on North Haven, which my mother canned and brought home.

We walked through sheep pastures to the north side of the island once to have a picnic at the water's edge on a small, stony beach. I kept picking up a foul odor the westerly wind was carrying toward us, so I walked along the shore, looking for the cause. I found two large carcasses, rotting away between some rocks. One was stripped to nothing but bones and the other had some of its flesh still on it. I did not know if they were sharks, or some type of whale. I did know, for sure, that they stank.

I had been told that one of Alfred's cows chased people who wore red clothing. I had my cousin's red coat on once when I climbed up the pasture fence to sit on the top rail. I heard hoof beats in the pasture, and I looked to see that cow charging in my direction. I jumped down, and ran and hid in the outhouse, afraid to come out for a while. When I did come out, the cow had her head down, eating grass, so I took the coat into the house.

Alfred had a lamb that followed us around like a dog every day, and was a nice pet. On a day we prepared to go home, they tied the lamb to a stake behind the house, so she wouldn't see us leave. She was not fooled, and cried steadily. She finally broke the rope, and came running around the house, coming to each one of us, still bleating nonstop. They had to drag her back out, under protest, to tie her back up.

We did not get back to North Haven for a couple of decades then, until the mid sixties. My family and I camped out in tents at Mullen's Head Park one year, but we found it cold at night, and uncomfortable sleeping on the ground. We later rented three different summer camps at Bartlett's Harbor, on three other vacations, and were a lot more comfortable. Once, at Bartlett's Harbor, my mother and one of my boys had rowed off in a borrowed boat without our knowledge. We saw the skiff drifting back into the harbor, with no one aboard. We didn't know if they were marooned on an island or what, but they managed to walk in after a few hours, exhausted. The boat owner let us know he was not happy that happened.

In the sixties, I bought a small parcel of land on the island, just below the standpipe, planning to build a small summer house there, so my mother could stay where she began her life. Before I bought that lot, I asked my aunt, who had eighty-eight acres on Southern Harbor, if she would sell me one acre. She said, "No, I ain't got to, and I ain't goin' to!"

My cousin, Bill Hopkins, owned a small ferry, which he used to transport as many as three cars at a time, and many walk-on passengers, across the Thoroughfare between North Haven and Vinalhaven, a distance of a little less than a half mile. Actor Robert Montgomery had a home at Kent Cove, and produced the television program, *Robert Montgomery Presents!* I was riding the ferry with Bill, when Mr. Montgomery came aboard for a ride to Vinalhaven, and Bill introduced me to him.

After I bought the lot at North Haven, the town passed a land use ordinance, and I was refused a building permit. Everyone I was referred to who had anything to do with enforcing the ordinance brushed me off in a stern, hostile manner. I began to realize that it would be futile for me to try to get established there, and I gave the land away so I would not be taxed further for a lot I would not be allowed to build on.

In 1983, my wife and I ferried to North Haven to attend my Aunt Kathleen Dyer Popp's 100th birthday at the Grange Hall. The ferry stopped running before the party was over, so we had a plane come over from Owls Head to pick us up at the airstrip, which was right behind the Grange Hall.

Some years later, I drove a busload of Damariscotta area senior citizens to the Rockland terminal, to board the ferry for North Haven, so they could have a picnic at Mullen's Head. A bus was furnished for us, so I could drive them around the island, and I showed them sights along the way that I thought might interest them. A Mr. Adams had supplied us with a large pot of hot coffee, and we enjoyed the picnic near the water's edge.

I have not been to the island since.

(The "Novie" boat, *Islander*, captained by Frank Lipovsky, did exist, and was used for carrying passengers and freight from Rockland to the islands around the start of World War II, and for a short while after.)

A Taste for Salt Water

The steamer *North Haven* was put into service on the Rockland-Vinalhaven-North Haven-Stonington-Swan's Island route in June 1931 by the Vinalhaven & Rockland Steamboat Company. Courtesy *North Haven News*

Built in South Portland in 1913, the steamship measured 103 feet, displaced 210 gross tons, with a 23.5 foot beam. Originally christened the *Electronic,* the steamer first ran trips in Nova Scotia, traveling between the Cape Breton cities of Sydney and North Sydney. Officials from the Vinalhaven & Rockland Steamboat Company sought out the steamship purchased it and sailed the ship back to Maine, where it began service in the summer of 1931 under its new name, *North Haven*. In his book *Steamboat Lore of the Penobscot,* author John M. Richardson wrote fondly about the *North Haven*, calling it an "able and fast stepping" boat. Richardson admitted the *North Haven* was never pursued for her beauty, but was genuinely admired for her smooth flowing power and her many conveniences. Richardson reported the 480-horsepower engine easily managed the traveling speed of 12 knots and "can readily be picked up well in excess of that mark when desired." The *North Haven* made the 40-mile journey from Rockland to Swans Island year round and Richardson praised "the roomy bow deck which will conveniently handle much freight and automobiles to boot." The raised pilothouse reportedly was the subject of ridicule but Richardson noted that Captain Ross Kent approved it, especially for the visibility. However, it was estimated the captain in his perch "travels an extra 10 miles on the 40-mile run of a rough day as that high-set wheelhouse arcs back and forth, for the *North Haven* is a deep roller. No place for a land lubber when there is a sea going". Despite her looks, the steamer was valued for efficiency and was especially known for being extraordinarily strong and sturdy in the ice. The *North Haven* displayed her abilities at navigating the icy Thoroughfare in this photograph. Perhaps this picture was taken during the winter of 1933-34 when the Thoroughfare froze for several months and prohibited steamship travel. With the crowd gathered at the steamboat wharf one could speculate that this was the *North Haven's* first stop there after a long winter with the Thoroughfare frozen. Several adventurous souls walk out on the ice, not far from steamer's narrow path through open water.

One of the best-loved local steamboats was the J.T. Morse, which operated for many years between Rockland and Bar Harbor as well as ports in between. Launched in 1901, she ran here until 1933, when she was sold to another shipping line and her name was changed to the Yankee. (Photo submitted courtesy Rockland Maine Historical Society)

A Taste for Salt Water

David Hopkins recalls one of his earliest memories at age three when he heard the crash of his grandfather Elmer's truck breaking through the aging steamboat wharf. As he looked over from his family's home above the old Hopkins' Store, David remembers seeing the truck precariously perched among the wharf's broken timbers. As the story goes, Elmer's oldest son, Emery, was backing his father's truck onto the wharf when it fell through a section of rotting boards. In the photograph, Emery is seen kneeling by the truck while Elmer approaches on the left. Reportedly, the *J.O. Brown* scow, formerly Dr. Weld's coal scow, was used to hoist the truck to level ground.

Elmer Hopkins was the oldest son of William and Lillian (Thomas) Hopkins. In 1923, he married Nina Cooper and they had five children, Emery, William, "Bill," Lyman, James, and Jeanette. The family lived in the house between the library and the Post Office, now owned by their granddaughter, Deb Graham and her husband David. Elmer took over his father, William's, woodcutting and ice businesses and managed a sawmill and several icehouses. In addition, Elmer did road building and earthwork, likening him to an Elliott Brown figure of today's time.

While repairs were made after Hopkins' truck broke through the wharf in 1956, it was evident that a major rebuild would be required. The dock originally belonged to F.H. Smith, proprietor of the nearby general store, which later became Waterman's. In 1911, the Eastern Steamship Company leased and lengthened Smith's dock and built a large freight shed and two slipways to accommodate the steamships that frequented the Thoroughfare. Then, during the Great Depression, the Eastern Steamship Company suffered financially and also faced competition from mainland trucking businesses. As a result, the company suspended service along the Maine coast in 1935. Although the wharf and freight shed were still used by local steamboats, the area gradually fell into disrepair. By the time of this photographed mishap in 1956, plans were underway to tear down the wharf and freight shed and fill land to create a parking area and build a dock for the new state run ferry, the *North Haven*, christened in 1960.

Thanks go to David Hopkins, Toot Waterman, Joe Brown, and Kenneth Hopkins for sharing information about the photograph.

—Lydia Brown, *North Haven News*, November 2012.

Hopkins' truck after breaking through the dock, November 8, 1956. Photo courtesy of North Haven Historical Society.

A Taste for Salt Water

The author's grandfather, Avery Dyer, mail carrier, in front of Waterman Garage, originally F.H. Smith's stable. Factory boarding house in background. Photo courtesy of North Haven Historical Society.

Born in August of 1874, [the author's grandfather] Avery Dyer was the oldest son of Erwin and Adella Thomas Dyer's six children. In 1894, he married Lottie Hopkins, daughter of Emery and Hannah Pierce Hopkins. Together they had six children, Alfred, Bernard, Rosamond, Ruby Mildred [Ruby Mildred Dyer Perkins, the author's mother], Evelyn, and Thorne. In the 1900 census, Avery noted his occupation as "hostler," defined as one who stables and cares for horses. Two of the village general stores, F.H. Smith and C.S. Staples maintained livery stables and it is possible that Dyer, pictured here in front of F.H. Smith's stable, tended the horse there. The presence of the boarding house in the background dates the photograph to the late 1890s, as the building was dismantled after the cannery shut down in 1897.

By the 1910 census, Avery Dyer reported his occupation was a mail carrier and in 1920 census he was a carpenter. Avery's youngest sister,

Kathleen Dyer Popp spoke of her brother's occupations in an interview with Eliot Beveridge.

"He loved horses: give him a horse and he was happy... Avery was a carpenter too, he carpentered. And Grandpa Dyer was a carpenter, so it's all in the family... Avery was the rural mail carrier, the first one they ever had, and he had his horse and wagon. In the winter he'd use a pung, a short stubby pung, and one horse... At the time I don't think it came every day, you know, only twice a week at first. He'd start off with the mail in the morning and he used to get back about three o'clock in the afternoon. Course, the horse wouldn't get him around as fast and there were a lot more stops than there are now, especially in winter."

Although free mail delivery is a convenience we can presently take for granted, its establishment nationwide in 1902 proved revolutionary for rural Americans. While towns of over 10,000 people received free mail delivery as early as 1863, rural residents needed to travel long distances or pay for private delivery in order to obtain their mail. Groups like the Grange, the National Farmers' Congress, and the State Farmers' Alliance lobbied the government to authorize funding for rural mail delivery. In addition, people across America sent over 10,000 petitions requesting the establishment of free mail delivery. Opponents to rural mail delivery claimed it would bankrupt the government and hurt merchants who relied on business from farm families when they made their weekly trips to town to get mail and do errands. Despite opposition, rural mail delivery proved successful and residents responded enthusiastically, as one Colorado woman remarked, she was happy to "have our mail fresh instead of stale."

Mail carriers, like Avery Dyer, were required to provide their own horse and buggy (or sleigh!). Essentially serving as traveling post offices, mail carriers sold stamps and money orders and offered news from town. In addition, they were asked to do errands and read or write letters for those unable to do so. During the winter and spring, mail carriers encountered roads impassable from snow and mud. In some rural areas, residents were motivated to build and repair roads and bridges in order to encourage regular mail delivery. During Avery Dyer's service as mail carrier on North Haven from 1903 to 1917, the island had two post offices, one at Pulpit Harbor and another at the Thoroughfare. The Pulpit Harbor post office closed in 1932 and reportedly some areas of the island still did not have rural delivery service until after World War II.

In 1913, the government established parcel post delivery in rural areas. The effect on the national economy was "electric," as mail order catalogs allowed rural residents to access goods that were otherwise not readily available. The Sears & Roebuck Company boasted they sold "four suits and a watch every minute, a revolver every two, and a buggy every ten." Mail order catalogs were nicknamed the *Homesteader's Bible* or the *Wish Book* and were considered one of the most important books in the farmhouse.

Accounts note the remarkable variety of items shipped by parcel post. A *Smithsonian* article, "Parcel Post: Delivery of Dreams," reported that prior to World War I even children were sent through the mail. In one such incident, the parents of four-year-old May Pierstroff in Idaho send their daughter to her grandparents across the state, all for the postal rate of 53 cents. Soon after, the Post Office Department banned sending humans by mail. In 1916, a dismantled bank was sent through the mail from Utah to California. The entire 80,000 bricks were shipped in 50-pound allotments, one ton at a time. The feat led the Postmaster General to rule that a single shipper could post no more than 200 pounds per day.

Avery Dyer, North Haven's first mail carrier, died in 1944 at age 70. Many thanks go to Jimmy Dyer and David Hopkins for sharing information on the Dyer family.

—Lydia Brown, *North Haven News*, December 2012.

THE YACHT *SARAH B.* COMES TO LYNN

Maybe back in the early forties, I heard my father telling someone about how the *Sarah B.* came to arrive at Lynn, Massachusetts. He said the treasurer of the Lynn Cooperative Bank, Charles Bethune, was travelling around Nova Scotia, maybe in the early thirties, and stopped in at a shipyard at Tiverton on the Digby neck. A sixty-three-foot double-ended hull was under construction there, and Charley was asking questions about it. He learned it was to be a fishing dragger. When asked what he would offer for it, he said, "I'll give you a thousand dollars for it." He came back to Lynn, thinking no more about it. A few weeks later, he got a phone call from the shipyard, explaining that the hull was being towed to Lynn, and asking where he wanted them to put it.

The great depression was on in full-swing at that time, but I often wondered how a hull of that size could be bought for such small change, even in that era. Perhaps the yard was losing money, and needed cash to pay the employees. Maybe they had a more lucrative contract to build another ship, and needed to get that one out of the way.

I don't know what stage of completion the hull was in when it arrived, or who finished it up, or exactly where. A French Canadian ship's carpenter, Jules Comeau, lived in the area, and was known as a fine craftsman with hand tools. He was well known around the Lynn Yacht Club. I suspect he did much of the finish work on the *Sarah B.*

Jules was a quiet, soft spoken man, and hearing him talk in his smooth accent was like listening to fine music. When he sailed with us, he was assigned a single bunk built just forward of the main bunk room, and aft of the forecastle. From that time on, it was known as Jules Comeau's bunk.

When the ship was completed, Mr. Bethune named it *Sarah B.* after his mother. He made a small model of it which he kept in his office at the bank.

At some point in the late thirties, Mr. Bethune sold the *Sarah B.* to my father, R. L. Perkins, Sr. He made a comfortable living around Lynn as a master plumber, having attended Wentworth Institute, and quickly passed both the journeyman and master plumber's exams. He bought the boat for recreational purposes, and expected to carry passengers for hire.

My parents separated around 1935, and my two brothers and I lived with our mother after that. We lived in a second floor apartment beside the Euclid Avenue School at the time, and then moved to Beverly, in 1937. We moved to South Hamilton in 1939, and lived there for quite some time. It was around 1938 or 1939 that we learned our father had bought the boat.

My father gathered a crew, mostly of his long time friends, who were usually available to sail on days and weekends off. Ray King, an executive of the Prime Manufacturing Company and my father's real estate partner, served as ship's engineer. Leon Hannon, an ex-Navy man, who worked at General Electric, served as a deckhand and helmsman. A man I only knew as Winship served as cook. I served as an apprentice seaman and helmsman.

Off and on, on summer vacations and weekends, my brothers and I would walk about six blocks to the Hamilton and Wenham train station. After boarding the train for Lynn in midmorning, the conductors who got to know us always asked us if we were going to work on our father's boat.

The first day we saw the *Sarah B.*, we got off the train on the elevated Lynn station in Central Square and walked down the steps to the street level where our father was waiting in his 1938 Nash Lafayette sedan. The back seat was removed and that area covered with plumbing tools, so some of us had to sit on tool boxes.

The yacht club was about a mile from the train station, on Washington Street. As the car rumbled over the granite cobblestones and streetcar tracks, we passed several brick shoe factories on the right hand side. My grandfather, Thomas Burton "Burt" Perkins was a prominent Lynn steamfitter from about 1900 to about 1935. Semi-retired with heart problems, one of the last jobs he had was running a large stationary steam engine that supplied the power to run the machinery in the whole cluster of factories.

On the left side, we passed my father's first plumbing shop at number 696. The Champion Mattress factory was next door. I remember that once the stitcher got his machinery set up and running, he would sing quite loudly and well, *Winter Wonderland*.

Next, our mouths watered as we passed the Niles Potato Chip factory. We thought those chips tasted better than all others. They were sold by the pound in Kraft paper bags. We passed a Studebaker garage, "Langille Motors," just before we got to the yacht club.

The Lynn Yacht Club was a large gray wooden building, with a few medium sized rooms in front, close to the street, and had a large boat building loft behind them, all at street level. Much of the space under the clubhouse contained storage lockers for the members' boating equipment.

We turned into the driveway beside the club, and proceeded downhill to the boat yard. We had to stop, get out, and unlock a chain link gate so we could get in. Once in the yard, we closed the gate, because only members were allowed in.

My father drove around the end of the clubhouse building, and, pointing to the huge double ended motor sailer sitting in its cradle built of ten by twelves, announced that it was his boat. We found it was the largest boat in the yard. Close to it sat a large, double ended power cabin cruiser, about fifty-five feet long. It was named *Laumar,* and its home port was listed as Rockport. Behind our boat, a V-bottomed cruiser sat in its cradle. My father said it was an old rum runner, and had airplane engines in it. Various other smaller boats were being worked on by their owners to get them ready for spring launching.

To get into the ship, we had to climb about ten feet up a wooden ladder to get on deck. My father unlocked the pilot house door, and my brothers and I spent some time walking through the ship, getting familiar with its layout. We were, naturally, fascinated with it.

The middle of the pilot house floor had two large trap doors that, when opened, allowed standing room around the engine for easier maintenance. While closed, those trap door deck surfaces displayed a large colorful compass rose inscribed with "North" pointing toward the bow.

I found the inscription "NET 20" carved into an overhead deck beam in the engine room, and asked my father what that meant. He said the ship was designed to carry twenty tons of cargo.

The Lynn Gas and Electric Company manufactured illuminating gas from coal in a plant across the harbor. The problem with that was, the wind usually blew from the plant toward the yacht club, continually covering the boat decks with coal dust. One of our first shipboard jobs was sweeping the decks every time we came aboard.

While my father busied himself with spring maintenance to make the boat ready for launching, we roamed the weather deck and were able to see some of the gas company's manufacturing procedures. A car full of coal was set afire, and shoved into an oven. The gas emitted was piped into the nearby gas holder, which looked somewhat like gasoline storage tanks, except that it was higher, and the top half moved up or down as the gas went into it or was consumed. Then, at the right time, a bell would sound, the flaming car was wheeled back out, and the fire quenched with water. The remaining product was called "coke", and was sold for boiler fuel. Occasionally we would see a small collier bearing a Scandinavian flag come in at high tide, and unload coal at the gas company dock.

The yacht club had a large closet that contained a nickel slot machine. We would watch people play it, and if they did not have any hits, my father thought that was the time we had the best chance of winning. He would give us a few nickels, and, between the three of us, one of us might make something like a six-to-twelve nickel hit. The janitor was watching us one day, and told us two men came in some time back and said they were taking the machine out for repair. He said he did not dare question the men because one of them kept his hands in his pockets, as though he might have been carrying a gun. Naturally, they never brought the machine back.

While my father kept himself occupied with the spring maintenance, we had to remind him when we were getting hungry. He would sometimes give us a few nickels and dimes, and send us up the driveway to the small convenience store next to it. Those stores were not much different than today's variety and convenience stores. The first products we were faced with coming in the door were the many racks of cigarettes behind the check-out counter. Once in there, we selected pies and cakes which could be bought for a nickel, or sometimes some cookies. Going back to the yard, if the gate had been closed, we had to holler to whoever might hear us and explain who we were so we could get back in.

Sometimes we were given a sanding job, to prepare a surface for repainting. If it was a spot not requiring too much expertise, my father let us paint it. Sometimes we were asked to scrape or sand some dried marine growth off the bottom, in spots that were missed during haul out.

Once, we had to remove the worn canvas roofing over the bunk room. We covered the exposed boards with a thick oil paint, so the replacement canvas would absorb it, and adhere to the wood. Then we stretched and tacked it down, trimming the edges, and fitting it around the skylight ventilator. Then, we coated the weather side with buff paint.

We had no leaks when we were done.

The *Sarah B.*'s harbor mooring was a 300-pound iron mushroom anchor, which had about twenty feet of chain shackled to it, and fifty feet of Manila line between that and the ship. In those days, Manila rope was about all that was available for that purpose. Since Manila was subject to rot and marine life boring, it was recommended it be renewed every boating season. One day, my father took us to a ship chandlery in Boston to buy a new mooring line. A salesman cut our 50 feet off of a coil, and instructed a rope splicer there to splice an eye on the mooring bit end, and a smaller loop was spliced around a metal collar so it could be shackled to the mooring chain. A skilled splicer is interesting to watch at his work.

We noticed a large two-bladed aircraft propeller hanging high on the wall in the warehouse. It seemed out of place amid all the nautical equipment.

Back at the boat yard, the mooring was assembled, piled on deck, and the mushroom hoisted and dangled off the bow.

On launching day, maybe late in May, we worked the ship over to the marine railway by towing it with cables wound up on a spool powered by an old car engine. We all laid out wooden rolls for the cradle to roll on. Once on the car, we lashed the cradle down tight, so it would not float off with the ship. While the tide was coming up, we painted the bottom with several gallons of green copper bottom paint. We timed the job so we would launch at high tide while the paint was still wet, as the manufacturer instructed.

When the tide was nearly high, someone started the cable pulling machinery, and gave the cable a few jerks so we could release the boat launching marine railway car holding dogs, and the ship was allowed to begin its roll into the harbor. A brake was applied to slow it down a little, causing that apparatus to squeal and give off a lot of smoke. When the car reached a stop at the foot of the rails, the tide was a couple of inches shy of floating us off, so I went down on the floats to wait it out.

It was a nice sunny day, with only a murmur of a breeze blowing. The sunlight sparkled off the fairly calm water, which made barely audible rippling sounds against the floats. I liked to walk around the floats, looking down through the clear greenish sunlit water, examining the bottom.

A woman appeared to be sanding some hatchway woodwork on a

deep-keeled sloop in the yard next to the embankment. I began to hear a series of loud thuds, like someone was sledging heavy timber. Looking that way, I wondered what was going on, then suddenly heard a sickening wrenching sound, and the cradle arm collapsed under the sloop, and it fell over on its side, landing with a loud "BOOM!" The girl lost her grip, and started sliding down the deck. There seemed to be no gunwales on that boat, and no railings. (Maybe it had one, but might have been removed to be re-plated or something.) The girl slid off the boat, and into the water below, which was about six-feet deep at that time. If it had been low tide, she would have fallen into the mud. A man appeared from behind the boat, and jumped in after her, but she did not appear to be in any trouble. They swam to a spot where they could climb out.

After the tide lifted the *Sarah B.* off its cradle, someone aboard threw us a couple of lines, and we pulled her backward and against the floats. We tied her up, and boarded to look for any water seeping into the bilges while waiting for any shrunken planks to swell. The aft hand-operated bilge pump was used a few times to expel it.

After finding no real problems, my father started the engine by hand flipping the flywheel and we cast off, heading for our mooring area. Once there, we lowered the mushroom, payed out all the line, and turned off the engine. We stayed aboard until we determined it was safe to leave the ship unattended. We got into the tender, which we had towed out when we left the float, and rowed in, wondering when we would sail somewhere.

Coming off the floats into the yard, a middle aged man crossed our path, carrying a large pair of well worn work gloves. I asked my father who he was, and he said his name was Mr. Gilbert. He said Mr. Gilbert was allowed to live aboard his boat near the edge of the embankment because he had no other home, in exchange for some work he did around the yard. His boat was a yawl, sitting in a cradle, and was about twenty-five feet long. It displayed dried out seams with cotton dangling out of them, and had a very high waterline. I doubted that boat would ever be launched again.

THE FISHING TRIPS

The *Sarah B.* made several recreational fishing trips. My brothers and I were allowed to bring a few classmates with us, who jumped at the chance to go. Sometimes one of the crewmen went with us, and sometimes a few of my father's other friends joined us. My grandfather came at least once, and Jules Comeau, the ship's carpenter, came a few times.

To go fishing, we would usually take a short cruise to a point about two miles off Nahant, and then drop our 60-pound yachtsman's anchor. We also carried two 100-pound anchors for overnight or emergencies.

The ship probably carried about eighteen or twenty deep sea hand lines wound on wood frames, and one pole. By the time we let the hand lines down to the bottom, they were nearly payed out to the limit, which was about 16 fathoms. We generally used clams for bait. After an hour or two, we generally had an adequate landing of cod and haddock. An occasional eel or dogfish we hooked were thrown back. Ground fishing was very relaxing, and we usually had good, sunny weather for it. I remember Jules Comeau, standing by the rail, holding his line, quietly puffing on his pipe, and looking pensively out to sea.

One day, while out there fishing, I climbed up on top of the pilot house, as I often did, to get a better look around. I noticed President Roosevelt's yacht anchored off Nahant, while he was visiting his nephew. A little while later, I watched it get up steam, haul anchor, and sail away to the southward. I watched it for some time, until it had gone by us. Then I saw the three-foot rollers from its wake approaching. I managed to hang on to the aft mast stay cable while we took the first one, but quickly dropped to a prone position, wrapping my arms around the horn, while I struggled to keep from being thrown off the roof from the violent rolling. I was more careful about standing up there, after that.

Sometimes, when we approached that same general area, we found mackerel or pollack running in schools near the surface. We rigged shiny lead-coated hooks and used feathered lures for trolling. We caught a lot of those species that way.

As long as there was no other boat traffic near us, my father let me handle the ship during the trolling, while he fished with the guests. One day, on one of those trips, my brother, Phil, insisted on taking the wheel, but he soon tired of it. My youngest brother, Bernie, did not want to be left out, so he demanded a turn also. He could hardly see over the wheel, and found out he couldn't do it either. I noticed the zigzag wake behind us, and straightened her out. There is a little knack to marine steering, and I had caught on to it quickly.

THE GRAVES LEDGE LIGHTHOUSE TRIP

One day, my father announced we would visit the Graves Ledge Lighthouse, about ten miles at sea off Nahant. We had never been in one, so we were excited about going there. Our group was made up of about four adults, and my brothers and me.

When we left Lynn, the sky was overcast, the seas calm, and vision limitless. When we got to the end of the channel, and turned a few degrees to port, we could just make out the lighthouse off in the distance.

After sailing about an hour, we arrived at the north side of the rock. We tied up to the mooring buoy, and the first group leaving the ship rowed to shore. A couple of us stayed behind, waiting for someone to row back for us.

During the wait, I heard the sound of airplane engines off in the distance, coming from the direction of Boston. As it neared, I recognized the dual-engine Fokker flying boat from the Winter Island Coast Guard Base at Salem Willows. The pilot was flying barely a hundred feet up, so he could get a good look at the lighthouse to see if anything was wrong. We exchanged waves, and the plane continued toward Salem.

When we were all on the ledge, we found ourselves on bare rocks, making up maybe three acres above water. The round granite light structure towered above us.

To get in, we had to climb about thirty-five feet up a brass ladder to get to the first opening. Above that, on each floor, there was a small window.

We were jittery about climbing so high up a ladder, but my father told us to take our time, hang on well, and don't look down. The keeper had seen us arrive, and stood by the open door waiting to grab us and pull us in when we got to the top of the ladder.

We found there were two men inside. They were glad to see us. I sensed it was a dismal spot to spend a lot of time, without seeing other people.

The keeper was happy to show us around. First, he explained how the mechanism that turned the light worked, and how it was maintained. He showed us a cistern that was once used to store drinking water, but

said it could not be used, because someone had spilled kerosene into it. I don't recall how they stored water after that happened.

Going up several circular stairways, we viewed a storage area, and circular living quarters. I noticed a lot of books displayed on shelves. It seemed there was little else to occupy one's mind while waiting for a break to go ashore.

The keeper took us out on the observation deck surrounding the light at the upper level. We could view miles of ocean from there. The keeper said that in bad storms, the waves splashed up to that height.

When the tour was over, we walked back down the stairways, climbed down the ladder, and rowed out to the *Sarah B*. We started the engine, cast off, and headed back to Lynn with the keepers watching and intermittently waving as we sailed away.

THE GLOUCESTER TRIPS

The *Sarah B.* made several trips to Gloucester. It was about a twenty-two mile trip from Lynn to where we tied up in the harbor, taking a good two hours of running time. On the first of those trips I made, we might have left Lynn around ten o'clock, and arrived a little after noon. We tied up at a wharf near the center of town, and our group had lunch in a dockside restaurant there. While waiting for our meals, my father slipped some of his charter advertising into the menus, but the owner was not amused, and took them out.

After spending an hour or two around the waterfront, we sailed back to Lynn, arriving at the mooring at about suppertime.

We tied up at Mello's wharf in East Gloucester a couple of times while I was aboard. The first time, some of us went ashore for a while, and a few of us stayed with the boat. If it was a very hot day, I enjoyed the shade of the pilothouse roof, and the breezes drifting through it.

The second time, we tied up at the dock at midday as usual. While we were discussing what we might do there, a big steel dragger, about eighty feet long, tied up abreast of us. A few minutes later, another dragger, about the same size, tied up next to the other one. There was hardly any breeze, and only a barely detectable sea surge. But, as little movement as those conditions caused, tons of pressure were compressing our wooden ship against the dock. After hearing several cracking sounds, we knew we had to get out of there fast, or be crushed. We backed out of that unsafe position, throwing the draggers' lines to a wharf man, and sailed to another wharf.

On one of our early Gloucester trips with a group of friends, we would sail around Cape Ann. After entering Gloucester Harbor, we steered for the Annisquam River, which separates the cape from the mainland. To enter the river, my father told an adult to take the hand held mouth horn and signal the cut bridge operator to open it up so we could go through. I asked my father to let me steer the ship through, but he refused. I could have done it, but he thought it was just too much responsibility for a kid my age. We did not use the ship's air whistle for that signal, because there were a lot of houses close by on the boulevard, and

The A. Piatt Andrew bridge spanning the Annisquam river at Gloucester, Mass.

The Breakwater Lighthouse at the Entrance to Gloucester Harbor

**Annisquam Lighthouse
Drawing by R. Laforest Perkins**

the loud blasts would make people jump, if they were not expecting it.

The Annisquam River is about four miles long, and we enjoyed the scenery we passed. About a half mile into the river, the railroad bridge was raised to let us through. Immediately beyond, the river made a sharp turn to port, and we went by the entrance to Little River. Turning to starboard, we passed Rust Island, where years later the A. Piatt Andrew Bridge was built connecting Route 128 with Gloucester's Washington Street. That was built high enough that any boat capable of navigating the river can do so without any fear of any masts coming in contact with it. Before that one was built, all vehicular traffic into and out of Gloucester had to go over the cut bridge on the boulevard.

From the Rust Island area, we passed marshland to port, and mostly residential housing to starboard. After about a twenty-minute run, we passed the Annisquam Yacht Club to starboard and Wingaersheek Beach to port, leaving the Annisquam Lighthouse behind as we entered Ipswich

Bay. Then, we had nearly a two-hour run ahead of us, to go around the Cape, and get back to the Gloucester Harbor area.

Standing on deck while we were cruising in Ipswich Bay, I heard my name called. My cousin, Kilton Brown, was in a small sloop we were passing, with a friend. I told my father we were hailed, and he brought the ship to a stop. My cousin came aboard, and he decided to cruise with us for the rest of the trip, and his friend sailed off toward Ipswich.

The weather breezed up as we passed by the entrance to Gloucester Harbor, and we had to travel parallel with the waves, which were mounting up to perhaps three or four feet high. We were taking such serious rolls that it was hard to stand up without holding on to something. Almost no one went out on deck, and I sat on the pilothouse seat which also served as an extra bunk, and which stretched from one side to the other. With my back against the port wall, and my legs flat on the cushion, I managed to stay in one place. My father had raised the jib, in an effort to steady the ship.

I never sailed in such a heavy roll before, and I was uneasy the whole time I endured it. I was relieved when we spotted the bell buoy at the entrance to the Lynn channel that day.

On another Gloucester trip, Charley Bethune, the ship's former owner, and a couple of other businessmen sailed with us. My father let me take the wheel as soon as we dropped the mooring line, to see how I handled the ship making a sweeping forty-five degree turn around the first beacon. He was pleased that I handled the job properly, and needed no correction. I steered for about an hour, changing course when my father instructed. Then, for some unknown reason, Bethune insisted my father take over, because he thought I was too young for the job. No one else ever complained.

We sailed through the Annisquam River, and into Ipswich Bay, cruising that area for the afternoon. The weather was fine, and the water smooth all day. As darkness approached, we started back upriver, deciding to anchor opposite the Annisquam Yacht club for the night. We dropped our one hundred pound anchor near the edge of the channel, and, because we were in a navigable waterway, posted a white kerosene lantern on our foremast for the night.

The adults sat around in the pilothouse, talking, and maybe playing cards. Having nothing to do, I felt bored, so I turned in on a lower bunk on the port side.

There were only one or two army style blankets on each bunk, so I crawled under a couple of them, and tried to sleep. I felt cold, because the overhead bunk room ventilator was left open, and the fuel compartment ventilator shaft was always open for safety reasons, creating a constant draft through the ship. If I managed to catch a few winks of sleep, I became aware of a throbbing sound approaching. The sound quickly magnified to a roar, and it sounded as if I was in its engine room as a dragger roared by our port side, to bring a load of fish to Gloucester. Then, hit by the dragger's wake, our boat rolled enough to shake me a little more awake. That happened on and off all night. Clearly, that was the wrong spot to set an anchor for the night.

The talking in the pilothouse went on for hours, until someone noticed they were out of liquor, so a couple of the men rowed to the yacht club, to go into town and look for some. I managed to get more sleep after that, and I woke up around daybreak. The ship was lying quietly at anchor, and I laid there for a few minutes, trying to decide when to get up. Then, I began to hear a slight thud, and the ship vibrated a little. Then, another, and a few seconds later, another. I decided about the same time as my father did, that we were touching bottom at low tide. My father quickly started the engine, hauled up the anchor, and moved the ship to a spot nearer to the yacht club. If only we had done that the night before!

Everyone was up by then, and we watched the sun come up over the horizon from the pilothouse. We also began watching a half dozen people digging clams in the flats beyond the channel, when Winship began serving up breakfast. He might have given us an orange or a banana, to start off with. In those days, orange juice only came in tinned cans, which took something away from the flavor, so we had none. Then, Winship handed up plates of hot fried egg sandwiches, fried in butter, and a pot of coffee.

Shortly after we had breakfast, we hauled anchor, and sailed upriver to the ocean, then headed back to Lynn.

THE HAPPY HOME BAKERS' EXCURSION

My father said he was going on a cruise to Scituate one day, and asked us boys if we wanted to go along. We had no idea where Scituate was, but, of course, we were excited about going.

After picking us up at the train station that day, he drove us directly to the yacht club, where we found our crewmen, Ray King and Leon Hannon, waiting for us. We learned that the *Sarah B.* had been chartered for the day by the Happy Home Bakers of Boston, and we were taking them from Lynn to Scituate and back, about a 21 sea mile trip each way.

My father and the crewmen rowed out to the mooring, brought the *Sarah B.* to the yacht club floats, and tied it up so we could load a few supplies aboard, which included a block of ice and two cases of soda pop my father had earlier picked up at the Moose Hill Tonic Company in Swampscott. My brothers and I planned to devour as much of that pop as possible on the trip. Then we all boarded and sailed across the harbor, tying up to an old abandoned pier where sailing ships used to come in and unload lumber and other goods in the old days.

Billy Yuill managed a gasoline station just up the street from there. He soon came with his tank truck, and filled our four 55-gallon tanks with regular gasoline. After he drove off, around midmorning, our passengers arrived in several cars. They parked on the pier, climbed down the ladder, and boarded.

Around ten A.M., we started our engine, swung around, crossed the harbor, and headed south in the two mile channel, which runs parallel with the Nahant causeway. We passed the Nahant Coast Guard Station, entered the open sea, and set our course for Graves Ledge Lighthouse, which was barely visible, about ten miles away.

The ship's 40-horsepower Palmer marine engine burned two gallons of fuel an hour, and pushed it along at ten knots, which made for leisurely, relaxing cruises.

It was a warm, sunny day when we started out, with calm seas, and excellent visibility. The passengers roamed about the decks, and engaged in group conversation for most of the trip.

After we passed Graves Ledge, the skies became a little hazy, but visibility was still good. When we had cruised for about another three quarters of an hour or so, having passed Boston Harbor, we went by Minot's Ledge Lighthouse, a big granite sentinel that was completely surrounded by water. I didn't know it then, but that lighthouse was a replacement for a previous one that was built supported by iron rods, and that had toppled into the sea just after midnight in a gale in the 19th century, costing two men their lives.

After running a few more miles, we swung into Scituate Harbor, and tied up to the town pier on an ebb tide a little after noon. The passengers scrambled up a ladder, and soon disappeared into town. The rest of us remained aboard, having a sandwich lunch, and trying to find something to keep us from being bored while we waited for the passengers to come back. There was not much activity, if any, while we were tied up there.

My youngest brother, Bernie, dropped a fishing line in the water, and came up with a small fish, about four inches long. My other brother, Phil, went below, and I sat around in the pilothouse, listening to the seagulls, and relaxing on the full-length cushioned seat which stretched about eight feet across the aft wall. I began to feel hot, and a little drowsy, the summer sun being right overhead.

Around midafternoon, I was jolted erect by a loud boom, a cracking sound and quivering walls, followed by a big splash off the starboard side. After I collected myself, I began to realize that some clown had jumped off the pier onto the pilothouse roof, then jumped ten feet through the air to the water below. My heart pounded for a while from the scare, and I was not amused. My father appeared from below, asked what happened, grumbled, and chided the swimmer.

The rest of the passengers had begun to return from town and when they were all aboard, we cranked up the Palmer and cast off. We backed away from the pier, swung around, and headed out of the harbor, encountering a light fog, which had begun to drift toward us in patches. We turned to port, and set a course for Minot's Light, passed it, and set the next course for Graves Ledge. A light breeze continued to blow the fog past us in patches, and, at best, our vision was reduced to a few hundred yards. In this cool, damp setting, most of the passengers hung around in the pilothouse, or went below to sit on the bunks and converse. The young fellow who had jumped into the water at the pier, was still walking around in his swim trunks and sneakers carrying my brother's fish in his hand.

I stood forward deck watch for much of the return trip, feeling a little uncomfortable in the chilly dampness. Somewhere off Boston Harbor. I spotted a ship, dead in the water, about five hundred feet off our port bow. It was almost an exact duplicate of our boat, except it was about twenty-five feet longer, and displayed a Canadian flag. She had heard our fog signal, and stopped for safety reasons, and because we had the right of way. We stopped our wheel, and signaled for it to proceed, so we could watch it go by. We exchanged waves, and she gradually disappeared into the fog, heading east. Then, we increased our throttle setting, and resumed cruising speed.

We could hear the Graves' powerful fog signal from miles away, gradually growing louder as we approached the ledge. My father said we would soon see the lighthouse off the starboard side. The fog opened up so we could see it for about five seconds, then closed back in. From there, we set our course for the gong buoy at the entrance to the Lynn channel, and after sailing another hour in thick fog, we picked it up at about suppertime. The fog had begun to lighten by then, and we could steer by the green lighted channel markers we were passing off the port side.

Entering the harbor, we glided across it at reduced speed, and tied up to the pier we had left that morning. As the Happy Home Bakers' group said goodbye, and climbed up the ladder to get to their cars, we hoped they enjoyed their trip, and went home happy.

THE REGATTA

Readying for a cruise one day, my father announced to me that we were going on a regatta. I didn't know what that meant, so he explained a large group of local yachtsmen had agreed to cruise to the same destination which, in this case, happened to be Salem Willows. We only had a few adults going with us, maybe only two or three. My brothers did not go with us on that trip.

I think we left Lynn Harbor sometime after noon. A few other participating boats could be seen at various distances ahead.

We had good weather, with a lot of clouds in the sky, and a mild breeze blowing. Rounding Nahant, we began to take a light roll. Off Lynn Beach, we began to take a little more active roll, and slowly overtook small sailing vessels and power boats.

A small power boat was running at near matching speed, about fifty feet off our port beam. My father and I were watching it through the pilothouse doorway, when the Slavic skipper, who had been drinking a can of beer, suddenly threw the empty can in the water, and, producing a .22 caliber rifle, quickly took a shot at it. Since the gun was aimed in the direction of our bow, my startled father jumped behind the pilothouse wall. I was startled, but did not move. The man raised both arms in the air, clutching the gun in one hand, as some kind of victorious expression that he might have hit the can. He saw we were not laughing, laid the gun down, and continued steering his boat.

It took us about an hour and a half to run about fourteen miles to Salem Willows. We maneuvered through some anchored boats, and dropped our 100 pound anchor, maybe a hundred feet off the big wooden pier there. We prepared and ate supper, and mostly just relaxed, while we waited for the fireworks scheduled to go off there after dark.

A replica of an old historical sailing ship, was tied up at the pier, and the fireworks would be launched from her deck. Around nine PM, up went the first shot, exploding in the air with a loud boom. The noisy and colorful display lasted probably about a half hour, and we found we were a little too close to it. Smoldering expended fireworks debris landed in several spots on our craft, and I continually walked the decks, picking them up, and tossing them into the water.

After the fireworks were over, I went below and turned in. We were boarded by someone I did not know and a lot of conversation piped up in the pilothouse, then I dozed off.

The next day, after breakfast, I got into our tender and rowed over to The *Arbella*, to get a closer look at her. Then, I rowed through the anchorage to look at the other boats, and around the landing.

The Willows is a small amusement center on a point of land nearly surrounded by water, and accessed by a dead-end street. On one side of the street is a row of businesses, including, in those days anyway, a Chinese chop suey sandwich shop, a "Dodgem" ride, a carousel, an arcade, a shooting gallery, a self-service photo booth, and a candy and ice cream shop. The area across the street was all green grass to the water's edge, with three good look-alike cottage style restaurants in one corner near the bay.

I must have lacked both money and interest that day, so I rowed back to our ship to await departure.

THE TOW JOB

The *Sarah B.* was returning from a trip one fine day. When we were coming around Nahant late in the afternoon as we aimed for the Lynn channel, someone aboard spotted a cabin cruiser with its flag flying upside down, and the people aboard waving. My father slowed our boat, turned it around, and maneuvered to come alongside.

The boat in trouble belonged to Mr. Newhall, who owned Newhall's Package Store in Wyoma Square in Lynn. His engine had stopped, and he could not restart it.

We threw Newhall a towline, and waited until he hauled his anchor. We slowly took up the slack, then applied full power, heading for the channel. The drag slowed us to about six knots, and my father sent a message to Newhall via a hand-held megaphone to put his transmission in neutral, thinking if his propeller spun free, it might relieve some of it.

Arriving at the mooring area by the last channel marker, we brought the two boats to a stop, and lashed the disabled boat alongside. We then proceeded to the club floats slowly, so Newhall could tie up there for the night. We let go the ropes and moved ahead, discharging our group on the floats. Then, we put the *Sarah B.* on its mooring at dusk.

THE SINKING

As I pointed out previously, it was recommended that boaters replace their manila mooring lines every year. One year, before launching preparations, my father inspected his line, and concluded it looked good enough to last another season.

The *Sarah B.* was moored on it for a while that summer, until a wind-whipped storm blew up one night. My father received a phone call explaining that our mooring line had parted, and the ship had drifted into the northern part of the harbor, and sunk. He drove to the location, and was stunned to see the *Sarah B.* resting in the mud, and up against a dock with only the masts and the pilothouse above water. He somehow got a line aboard and tied her to the dock so it would not float away, then waited for the tide to go out, trying to decide what to do next.

When the tide went out, he bored some holes in the bottom of the hull, to let the sea water out. While doing that, a man I will call Bill D. approached, and offered to help him. While the water was running out, an inspection revealed several punched holes in the starboard side. The ship had banged against a large bolt sticking out of the dock, punching only one hole below the water line. But, as the ship began to fill and sink down, a series of other holes were punched, and the boat filled faster, and sunk more quickly.

My father picked up some canvas, wooden slats, and small nails, and he and his helper made patches and covered the holes after the water had run out. The tide came in and refloated the boat, but it was inoperable because the engine was still full of water. The ship was towed to the yacht club floats, and its cradle was lashed to the marine railway car.

After the cradle was submerged, the ship was pulled into it, hauled out, and winched to its usual yard position.

I did not participate in the hull repairs until they were in the final stages, but my two brothers spent a few days helping my father with that. When the damaged hull planks were removed, it was discovered that the ship had fir ribs in it and some were quite rotted, presumably because that area had finish planking on the inside, and moisture collected in those cavities, and could not get out. So a lot more planking than expected had to be removed, and oak ribs steamed and bent for replacements. By the time I got to help on that job, the planking was done, and I got to fill some of the fastening holes with dowels, cut them off, and sanded the area smooth, repainting the repaired section with the hull's traditional black enamel.

It took considerable time to clean up the sediment inside the hull, and to clean out the carburetor, engine oil pan, and replace its oil. Two double and three single mattresses were taken to an Eastern Avenue cleaning firm, and it was weeks before we could get them back out. The five six-volt storage batteries had to be replaced, and the battery charger had to be serviced. The cork life preservers and sails had to be dried out. The gas stove had an enameled cast iron top on it and must have been somewhat porous because little spots of enamel popped off, leaving a pock-marked appearance. The sinking was very costly, and the ship was out of service for much of that summer.

We were driving in the area near where the sinking had taken place when we were hailed by a man on the sidewalk. It turned out to be Bill D. and he was demanding payment for his assistance in raising the boat. When my father learned he was demanding fifty dollars for a day's work, he was distressed. In those days, most people were probably lucky if they earned twelve to twenty dollars a week, but Bill pressed his demand for fifty dollars and threatened to sue my father for it, so my father reluctantly gave in and wrote him a check for that amount.

THE PROVINCETOWN TRIPS

The *Sarah B.* made at least two Provincetown trips that I am aware of, with most of its crew and a few guests.

When the ship arrived at Provincetown one day, my father pulled in to a large pier, and tied up. Someone came running out of an office, and said he could not tie up there. My father demanded to know why not, and the man said the space was reserved for the Boston to Provincetown passenger ship. Then he told him to take a look behind him. The big ship was rounding the end of the pier, and so our boat was moved, pronto.

On one of those trips, a hurricane approached while our ship was anchored there. My father set out all of his anchors, and successfully rode out the storm. He stayed up all night to make sure the lines held, and the anchors didn't drag. The next day after the wind had abated, the anchors were weighed, and the ship started back to Lynn. Rounding the point outside the harbor, the waves started to build up, but not too bad, at first. A Coast Guard plane appeared, and waved to our boat. My father presumed it was just a friendly greeting, so he waved back, keeping to his course. The pilot had meant for him to turn back.

Although the hurricane winds had abated, the ocean waves had not died down much. Soon, my father found himself caught in the roughest seas he had ever seen, but did not dare to try to turn the ship around. He took the waves "quartering" all the way back. Some of the passengers were seasick, and probably not a little frightened.

The ship's fuel tanks were only standard 55-gallon steel drums, and the half full ones took a noisy pounding from the fuel sloshing from end to end. Custom approved fuel tanks have perforated baffles in them to prevent heavy surges. Fortunately, the *Sarah B.*'s tanks did not rupture or dislodge.

Approaching Nahant, the officer in charge of the Coast Guard Station there came out to meet them in their small power boat, wanting to know why my father was out in such bad weather. My father made light of it, and when he took his license examination, the official sent a letter to the reviewing board, saying, "I have seen Mr. Perkins operating in fair weather and foul. I strongly recommend that he be issued his license." He received it, and posted it in the pilothouse.

DISASTER: THE DROWNING

Occasionally, my father would row friends out to the *Sarah B.* at its mooring in the evening, and other times trips were not scheduled. He might offer them a complimentary highball, start up a card game, or discuss an upcoming fishing or excursion trip with interested parties.

On one such evening, my father brought a prominent Lynn building contractor and a woman I did not know aboard. I have no idea what went on that evening, except my father said he was showing them the boat.

When they left, my father pulled his round bottomed tender alongside, and the three prepared to get in. It was dark, but usually a little light from the Nahant causeway street lights and beach-going vehicles reflected across the water enough that boaters could at least dimly see what they were doing there.

My father got into the tender first, and steadied it, while helping the woman to get in. After she sat down, the contractor, who may have weighed two hundred and fifty pounds or more, must have slipped off the rub rail, and fell on the side of the tender, causing it to capsize suddenly, catapulting my father and the woman so deep under the ship they never touched the keel that extended five feet down at that point. The terror stricken woman somehow found my father in the underwater blackness, and got her arm around his neck in a stranglehold. He broke her hold, and pulled her to the surface, on the opposite side of the ship. He helped her toward the bow, and instructed her to hold on to the mooring line, while he swam around, looking for the contractor. He could make out muffled cries, but could not make out where they came from. He heard him say, "I'm going!" Then he heard nothing more after that.

As boaters became aware of what was happening, they picked up the survivors, and searched for the contractor. Someone towed the upturned tender to the floats, but no one could lift it out of the water. When enough men arrived to lift the tender out, the contractor was found lifeless under it, with his arm locked around a thwart. He must not have known how to swim, and must have been overcome with fear.

THE ALTERATIONS

My father decided that the *Sarah B.* might handle better if it had more weight in the bow. In the spring, while the ship was cradled in the boat yard, he took up the floor boards in the forecastle and prepared to add lead ballast. Being a plumber, he accumulated a lot of old leaky lead pipes and traps he had taken out of homes and replaced with copper, brass, or iron piping.

When any of us had any spare time at the plumbing shop on Eastern Avenue we would fire up a gasoline torch under an iron lead pot, cut up pieces of old lead, and melt them down. Drain-sludge sediments that had dried inside the pipes, gave off a lot of smoke and flames during the melting, and had to be scooped off and discarded when burned to ash. This work was carried on near the double doors, which were kept wide open for ventilation. The molten lead was ladled into a cast iron cupcake mold. When the lead hardened, the mold was turned over and lifted off the cakes, so they could cool and be stacked until we had enough for a trip to the yacht club.

On weekends, with my father, my brothers and I loaded the lead cakes into his Nash Sedan, maybe 200 pounds at a time. Then, we drove to the yacht club with the load.

One of us went down into the forecastle, one stood on deck, and two threw the lead up, a cake at a time. The deck man caught it, and dropped it down to the inside man, who dropped it into the bilge. It took a little time, but we probably handled a couple of loads a day.

When the lead was all in place, maybe a half-ton, we put the floor boards back. We climbed up the ladder, closed the forecastle hatch cover, and padlocked it. No one paid any attention to the teenager who was standing nearby, watching the whole operation. Maybe a week later, we climbed up on deck. When my father went to unlock that hatch, he found some splintered wood, and cursing, said that the ship had been broken into. We found that the lead had all been stolen.

We did not have enough lead to replace what was stolen. My father had a few old soapstone sinks he had removed from houses that he had upgraded to enameled iron ones. So, he cracked those up, and someone helped him load those pieces into the bilge. He said no one would steal old soapstone.

It was eventually discovered that the teenager who had been watching us was responsible for the theft. I don't think the lead or its cash value was ever recovered. My father thought the lead was tossed over a narrow fence between two buildings to an accomplice, but since the teenager was related to a yacht club employee, I think he got hold of a key and probably drove right out the gate with it.

About 55 years later, I was talking to a man taking photos in a shipyard in Thomaston, Maine. From what he said to me, I knew he was the thief. When I told him who I was and about my father's boat, he winced and began edging away from me.

One time, while the *Sarah B.* was under way, the engineer came up to the pilothouse to tell my father to pull in somewhere before they sank. He said he had all of the pumps running, and the water was up to the engine flywheel. I don't know anything more about that story, but I remember seeing the ship on a marine railway in a yard on the Saugus River. I suspect that the stuffing box packing had given out, and the ship had to be hauled to remedy that problem.

My father redesigned the bearing block. A heavier bronze casting was made, and a length of one-and-a-half inch red brass pipe was threaded into it. The stuffing box was moved inside, on the end of the pipe, at about waterline level. It never leaked again. A lignum vitae shaft bearing was dovetailed into the new housing. Skeptics said that job couldn't be done that way, but they were wrong.

A new bronze rudder was also cast, and the wooden one replaced.

SHORT, SHORT STORIES

When my brothers and I were around the *Sarah B.* when it was not under way, we were always looking for a way to amuse ourselves, to keep from being bored.

While I was standing on deck at anchor one day, two old 1920's era biplanes began circling the harbor a few hundred feet overhead. When they neared out boat, I went into the pilothouse and sounded a short blast on our horn. Then I jumped back outside just in time to see the pilot of one stick his arm out of the cockpit and wave. At that age, planes always excited me. My father had taken us up for our first ride at Beverly Airport when it was only a snow covered grass field around 1938 and it did not have paved runways.

One day while I was walking along the deck at anchor, Ray King came leisurely drifting by, sailing his gaff-rigged Hustler and shouted a message to me for my father. I didn't catch it all, and when he started to repeat it, his boat heeled over so far that I lost sight of him, his mast, and his sail. The centerboard came out of the water, and I thought water must have been washing over the coaming into the cockpit. He managed to right it slowly, and did not appear to suffer any ill effects, but it was startling to witness one of those incidents that happen so quickly and could prove disastrous.

Other members had built one-design Hustlers in the yacht club loft, and I once watched a group of them screwing planks to an upside down frame of one and wishing it was mine.

One day, while my father busied himself below deck, my brothers and I took the tender, and rowed over to the beach. After landing, we took off our shoes and socks, rolled up our pants, and began wading around in the water. We became tense when Bernie suddenly let out a yell, saying he had cut his foot. He might have stepped on a sharp seashell, or a piece of discarded glass, which caused a serious gash under a big toe.

We put him in the stern seat with his feet dangling in the water (the wrong thing to do, we found out) and rowed quickly back to the *Sarah B.* My father tied a cloth around his toe and, as fast as we could, got him to my father's doctor, who fixed him up. That was not a good day for us.

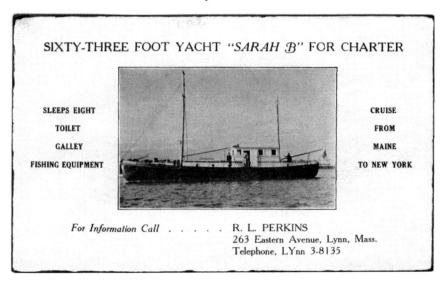

We were following the 55-foot rounded bottomed *Laumar* back to Lynn Harbor one day, while I was at the wheel. Things were going smoothly until, all at once, about halfway down the channel, I saw through the *Laumar*'s cabin windows a lot of sudden movement on deck. A group of wise guys feeling mischievous made a sudden dive to the starboard side, upsetting its balance so much that it rolled over down to the scuppers. After hanging in that position for a few seconds, it finally righted, and rolled over almost as far to port, and then began to stabilize. That gave me a good scare because if it had rolled to the point that it took on a lot of water and swamped, it might veer to one side while it slowed and grounded. Would I have had time to slow our boat, and take evasive action before we collided or grounded? If someone had fallen over the rail, he might not have known how to swim, or been run down. I learned at a young age how stupid it is to engage in horseplay around boats or to sail without all of the required safety devices.

Once, out at sea a considerable distance from shore, the *Sarah B.'s* engine started skipping, and shortly stopped. My father went down to the engine room, and found that the magneto, which supplied the electricity for the spark plugs, had overheated and stopped producing electricity.

The magneto was removed from the engine and taken apart. It was found that the heat had melted the insulating shellac inside it, and had gummed up the inner components. They needed alcohol to dilute the shellac so it could be removed. Not having the type that is normally used

The Sarah B. under full sail in Massachusetts Bay

for that, they dipped the parts in whiskey. The magneto was cleaned up enough that when reassembled, it worked well enough so the ship could make port. The magneto was again removed and taken to a shop that professionally rebuilt it.

One day, while the ship was in its cradle in the yard, I went down to the engine room to amuse myself, while my father did some work in the pilothouse. I decided to pretend I was going to start the engine by grabbing the flywheel, and trying to turn it over. It was not easy to do that, bucking the cylinder compression, even when I pulled the compression release lever. I would almost go by the compression stroke, but couldn't quite make it, and rolled it back to try again. In the meantime, I kept hearing the engine vacuum sucking in fuel each time and, on the last try, I heard the magneto click, followed by a loud bang, and the engine took off with a roar. Someone had left the ignition switch on, and I didn't know it. I scrambled up the ladder in fright, while my father walked over to the switch, and turned it off. I looked at my father, expecting some sort of reprimand, but he didn't say anything. In re-telling the story, he laughed at how frightened I looked.

One morning, my father took me to see Charley Bethune at his house in downtown Lynn, to look at a project he was working on. We found him in his cellar, building a round-bottomed boat he claimed to have designed. It was still upside down, and seemed to be near completion. There were piles of pine shavings, and pieces of wood scattered around the room. I asked Charley where it all came from, and he informed me that when you build a boat, about a third of the lumber winds up as waste.

I think the first time Charley took the boat out for a sail, he lost control and it tipped over. When he told us about it later, he said a friend told him, laughing, that he designed it and built it, but he couldn't sail it. Then, Charley burst out laughing.

The *Sarah B.* made many trips that I only heard little bits about later. One of the longest was when it sailed to Nova Scotia. The crew went, but I don't know who else. They stopped at Rockland, Maine on the way up, and visited my aunt there. I used to hear my father discussing the lighthouses, and other landmarks they passed on the way.

Some of my schoolmates and I were talking with Leon Hannon once about that trip. He said that on the day my father decided to start back from Nova Scotia, it was very foggy. One of the local men told him not to try it because he had to go through a narrow opening in a breakwater, and make a difficult turn in a certain spot after he passed it. Leon said my father did not want to wait until the fog lifted, so he navigated through it, and they never saw a thing until it lifted later at sea. I was always amazed at my father's navigational capabilities, considering he only had a ship's clock, a good Ritchie compass, and sets of charts to work with. He had no radar, depth sounder, ship-to-shore radio, or any other electronic equipment in use today.

When World War II erupted in 1941, it created problems for boat owners because by about 1942 gasoline was rationed. Commercial fishermen could buy gasoline because that was considered an essential occupation. But, since the *Sarah B.* was considered a pleasure yacht, my father could not get fuel ration stamps. He approached the Coast Guard to see if they could use the ship for coastal patrol or maybe transportation for wartime supplies. He was told they were interested, but the rating he would start out at would not cover his expenses. Since a boat that size is expensive to maintain even if it is not being used, my father decided he would have to advertise it for sale. My brothers and I were devastated.

In 1942, or thereabouts, a firm in the Great Lakes area contracted to buy the *Sarah B.,* delivered. My father removed the masts and lashed them to the deck so the ship would clear the bridges over the Erie Barge Canal. This last voyage took him across Massachusetts Bay, through the

Cape Cod Canal, through Buzzards Bay, past Long Island to New York City. Then, he proceeded north, up the Hudson River, into the Erie Barge Canal, across Oneida Lake, to a destination in Lake Erie, bringing our adventures on the *Sarah B.* to a close.

I still have many fond nostalgic memories of the *Sarah B.* One thing that I remember most, was returning from many of our trips at dusk or after dark, and cruising down the Lynn Channel past the several blinking green markers off our port side, looking at the lights at Revere Beach and the brightly lighted General Edwards Bridge. The passengers and crew, although a little tired, joyfully sang *Harbor Lights*, and *Red Sails in the Sunset*. I was not all that enthusiastic about approaching our mooring after those trips because that was the end of so many enjoyable cruises for me. After we tied up, I once told my father I could have sailed all night, and he just laughed.

While delivering the *Sarah B.* to Lake Erie, the ship ran aground on a sand bar in the Hudson River. The bar was fairly flat and free of rocks, and the ship made a slow, soft stop from full speed. My father noticed the ship had slowed down, and looking over the side, he could see the river bed. Checking his chart, he found the channel made a loop close to the shore, and did not notice the buoy in that position.

My father ordered anything heavy that could be moved to be placed as far forward as possible to drop the bow and lift the stern where the keel was deepest. Then, he instructed a crewman to take a kedge anchor in the tender and row as far astern as he had rope for, and drop it.

A speedboat was approaching, so just as its wake was rocking the *Sarah B.*, my father ran the engine up to full speed in reverse while the crew pulled on the anchor rope, and the ship backed off of the bar. He got the ship back in the channel, and resumed cruising speed.

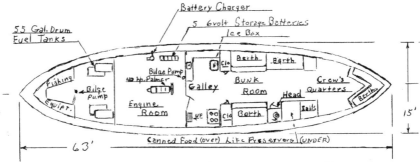

Lower deck diagram, Yacht Sarah B., Home Port, Lynn, Mass., Captain R. L. Perkins, Master

SALT WATER CAMPING

In the early forties, George Grant, a neighbor at South Hamilton, Massachusetts, occasionally took me with his family to their camp at Great Neck in Ipswich. It was a shell of a structure, built on wooden posts on a salt water cove between Eagle Hill and Great Neck. It was a wonderful place to swim, the invigoratingly cool water being barely over one's head on the far side at high tide. George's boy Donald and I spent many hours swimming and wading there, and rowing around Eagle Hill, exploring the small rivers that cut into the marshes.

In midsummer, 1944, I had been working in the shipping department at the local Sylvania plant. I took a week off and rented George's camp for ten dollars. He usually rented it for fifteen dollars a week, so I got a bargain. I took a school mate with me, a boy I also worked with on a kindling wood truck. We spent much of each day in the water. Some of that time, we stood in the mud while the tide was coming in watching four- or five-inch minnows nipping our toenails in a few inches of water.

It may have been that summer that George found a small eight-foot flat-bottomed boat that had a three-quarter horsepower air cooled Briggs and Stratton engine in it that he bought for Donald. The engine turned a propeller shaft when a v-belt on pulleys was tightened by a lever-actuated idler pulley. We got a lot of enjoyment out of it and it was relaxing not having to row.

In the winter, we took the engine out of the boat and used it to power two ice boats we had built. I carved a propeller out of a spruce two by four, which allowed us to reach speeds of about 10 to 15 miles an hour.

The camp had a nice porch facing the water, and we enjoyed eating clams we dug there, taking advantage of the cool evening breezes that drifted across it and watching many colorful sunsets at the end of the day.

Unfortunately, at the age of eighteen, in 1949, Donald was killed while rounding a curve at high speed on his motorcycle, about a mile from his home. The tires ran over some sand, causing the bike to flip. He was thrown to the ground, and hit his head on a rock. He died in the ambulance on the way to the hospital.

TROOP SHIP EXPERIENCES

I was drafted into the Army on February 8, 1946, and received eight weeks of infantry basic training in a heavy weapons company at Fort McClellan, Alabama. I was sent home on a week's leave before proceeding to Fort Lawton, at Seattle, to prepare to ship out to Japan. Maybe near the end of May, I boarded the 600-foot Navy troop ship *General Mann*, and was assigned a bunk on the first deck below the weather deck, in the aft section. We were not allowed in the bow section at any time.

After stowing my gear, I went on deck to look around the dock area. When I looked over the side, I felt quite high up off the water. In a few days, I would wish the sides were higher.

Late in the afternoon, the ship backed away from the dock, and steamed through the harbor toward Puget Sound. Maybe twenty minutes later, the ship came to a stop, and a ladder was dropped over the side. A small boat approached, and two soldiers who must have missed the ship at the pier, climbed aboard.

The ship continued on through the Sound, and headed toward the open sea. I looked long and hard at the land we were leaving, as it gradually disappeared from sight. That gave me a sinking feeling, and I wondered when, and even if, I would see it again.

For the first three days, we made steady progress, in fairly smooth seas. The men played cards and crap games for money, if they did not have galley duty.

About three days out, we ran into a typhoon, which lasted about three days. That was when I discovered the sides of the ship were not too high off the surface after all. As the ship heaved and rolled, the tops of the waves we cut through were higher than the weather deck. As the waves crested, the tops blew off under the strong winds.

This was a nerve jangling experience. As the bow sunk into a trough, the ship flexed, and the stern raised up in a series of sharp jerks. We looked over the side at the fantail, and we saw the wheels come out of the water down to the shafts they turned on. The wheels were rotating at maybe about 25 rpm, just enough to keep the ship pointing into the wind. I thought the wheels had a diameter of about 16 feet. As each

The 600 foot troop ship Admiral Eberle at San Francisco about late March, 1947

blade slammed down on the sea, it shook the ship, causing pipes to jangle in their hangers.

During this storm, the men I conversed with on deck gradually began to disappear. I found they were so seasick, they could not get off of their bunks. It looked to me at one time that three quarters of the men were sick. I saw men lying on the deck throwing up, and not moving. I only felt dizzy and I had a headache.

One day, during the storm, we were given hard boiled eggs and whole oranges for breakfast. We had to stand at raised tables to eat. Many of the men were too sick to eat when they got to the tables, and their rations were rolling back and forth on them. I caught a lot of that rolling food and shoved it into my pockets to eat later.

We were told the ship had drifted backwards over a hundred miles during the storm.

For the next week, the seas were relatively calm and we made steady progress. I only had to work in the galley two or three times. When I had to help pick up meat or vegetables for the day's meals, I was amazed at the box-car size of the coolers.

It was hard to keep clean in the galley, and our fatigue uniforms got soiled from greasy liquids that splashed on them.

One day, we took potatoes out of the mechanical peeler too soon. The chef found a few eyes left in them, and he made us run the whole batch through again. When we washed the china, if he found spots on two or three dishes, he made us wash hundreds of them all over again.

I thought the food on the ship was good, and I ate lots of it.

We passed another ship going in the opposite direction one night. It was so dark, we could not see it. Both ships sent messages for a while, using bright signal lights.

One day, while exploring other decks of the ship, I heard machinery running in a room in the stern. I found I had stumbled on the rudder control room. The rudder shaft had a yoke bolted to it, and double action hydraulic rams were mounted on each end of it. A large, constantly running electric motor drove the hydraulic pump, which pressurized and moved the rams in either direction to turn the rudder when activated up on the bridge. A standby electric motor sat idle, ready to take over, if the one in use failed.

One G.I. came down with meningitis, so we were all made to take sulfa pills. Arriving at Yokohama Harbor just after dawn, one day, we saw a few Japanese ships sitting in the mud, where they had been bombed by the U. S. Air Force. As our ship slowed to a stop, waiting for the tugboats that would assist us in berthing, scows propelled by one man using a sculling oar came alongside to pick up some of our garbage. When a Japanese tugboat came alongside to push us into the pier, a few soldiers hollered at the captain in imperfect Japanese, and he answered them in perfect English. In Japan, I was assigned to Service Troop, First Cavalry Division, Twelfth Regiment, at Camp McGill, in Takeyama. That camp was formerly the Nagai Naval Base. After serving as a guard for a short while, I was transferred to the motor pool, doing Jeep and truck maintenance until my time was up.

Late in March 1947, I was sent to a depot near Yokohama prior to boarding the ship that would bring me back to the United States. We were lounging around on cots, waiting for buses, when the worst earthquake I experienced in Japan struck. The room was lighted by bulbs screwed into sockets which hung down about three feet on wires. As the earth rumbled, the lights swayed, the building shook, the plastered walls cracked, and we bounced a little bit on our cots. After it subsided, we were herded into buses, and driven to the docks.

We could see our ship off in the distance. It was the 600-foot *Admiral Eberle*. The *General Mann* was painted battleship gray, but this one was more colorful. The ship's hull was gray, but the superstructure was white, had buff stacks and trim, and was manned by the Merchant Marines.

I was quartered on the first deck below the weather deck, in the bow section. I noticed a few little differences in the construction of the two ships. For instance, the deck supports on the *General Mann* were round steel columns, and those on the *Admiral Eberle* were I-beams.

After we put to sea, we ran into a snowstorm a few miles out, but the weather was relatively good for the rest of the trip. We had the misfortune of having to travel between the waves much of the time, and had to endure a lot of heavy rolling. One night, I was nearly dumped out of my bunk when the ship rolled sharply to starboard. It went over so far, it hung in that position for a few seconds, and I feared another big wave would roll us over, but the ship then rolled sharply to port, finally became more stabilized,, and took more moderate rolls.

As we approached San Francisco, most of us went up on deck as the Golden Gate Bridge came into view. We had slowed to about three knots. As I looked aloft, it seemed our mast might not clear the bridge, but it did. When the ship was directly under the bridge, the soldiers let out thunderous cheers, which were probably heard all over the bay.

After tying up, we went from the ship to Oakland Army Base to await transportation by troop train to Fort Dix, New Jersey, where I was honorably discharged in early April.

THE HERMIT OF PLUM ISLAND

I can't accurately remember when this adventure took place, but my guess at this time is that it probably happened around the mid fifties.

One summer day, an honorably discharged war veteran named Jack Helfand of Chelsea, Massachusetts, constructed a raft on the Rowley shore. It was about ten feet long, box shaped, and two by fours were nailed to the front to give it a pointed bow. It had a two by four for a mast, but I never knew it to carry a sail. Spaces in the frame revealed the whole thing was filled with sealed cans, pieces of cork, blocks of wood, and plastic jugs—anything that could be used for floatation. Only by a stretch of the imagination could this craft be thought of as seaworthy.

At some point, Jack pushed his craft into the Rowley waterway and headed toward the Parker River, probably using a paddle. In the river, he drifted past Grape Island, and the Ipswich Yacht Club at Great Neck, on the opposite side. Nearing the southern end of Plum Island, he landed on the beach, and his salt water journey came to an end at that point. If he had gone beyond that point into the open ocean, it is likely he could easily have been lost at sea. Once ashore, Jack proceeded to dig a cave in a sand dune above the beach. He was to live in that cave for about a year.

The local newspapers began carrying a few stories about Jack. They said curious beachgoers enjoyed talking to him, giving him things to eat, and swapping recipes. The papers quoted Jack as saying he landed there because he was "shipwrecked". Some people speculated that he intentionally landed at that spot. Jack tried to earn money by selling paintings he did on canvas and seashells.

One sunny afternoon, I decided to drive to Plum Island to see Jack. He had built a small fireplace of rocks on the sand in front of his cave. Water boiled in a can at the edge of the fire. I introduced myself, and Jack handed me a cup of coffee. I asked him how he happened to land at that spot, and he answered in one word, "Shipwrecked". I could not get him to elaborate further. Beachgoers continually came by to ask him a question or two.

Late one evening, about an hour before dark, I stopped by to talk to Jack again. We talked until after the sun had gone down, and only a small ray of light was visible in the west. When I could just barely see Jack in the darkness, I said goodbye to him and started back toward where I had left my pickup truck. Jack went into his cave.

I climbed over the sand dune at the edge of the beach, but, as I headed down the other side, I found I had waited too long to leave, and I was in total darkness. The stars were not even out. I lit a couple of matches, but they were totally useless in that expanse of darkness. I seemed to be on the path leading to the road, but I kept bumping into some brush which I had to go around. I hoped I did not get too far from the path, and that I wasn't becoming disoriented.

When the ground seemed a little smoother and clear, I assumed I had found the road, so I turned left, toward where I had left my truck. I walked slowly, with my hands stretched out in front of me, hoping I would not veer enough to one side to go past it. After a few more minutes, my hands came in contact with the tailgate, and I breathed a sigh of relief. I groped my way around to the door, and stepped in. It was great to get the truck started, and turn the lights on. I slowly turned it around, being careful not to back off the edge of the road, and headed back home.

The southern end of Plum Island is uninhabited, so I felt a little uncomfortable driving the six or seven miles in that desolate area, hoping my truck would not break down and leave me stranded until daybreak or later. I was glad when I reached the lighted paved road.

Newspaper stories revealed Jack stayed in his cave all winter that year. Someone from around Newburyport, who owned a Jeep with a snowplow on it, made weekly trips all winter, checking on him, and brought him some supplies.

A Miss Comeau I once knew, on North Ridge Road at Great Neck, showed me a painting Jack had given her because she had brought him food. It was a picture of deep purple or magenta colored drapes, which Jack had done on canvas, and entitled it "Tapestry". It was very colorful, and I would like to have owned it.

The following summer, Jack abandoned his cave, and I understand he went back to Chelsea. I never heard any more about him.

THE HERMIT OF GRAPE ISLAND

When I wrote the story of the Hermit of Plum Island, I had forgotten that another hermit existed almost within hailing distance on the closely positioned Grape Island.

In my early travels around Great Neck and Plum Island, Ipswich, I had always thought that Grape Island was part of Plum Island, the separation not being clearly visible when passing by.

Grape Island was a small, but thriving community of fishermen, farmers, and clam diggers, until the land was purchased by the U.S. Government and turned into a wildlife refuge in the middle of the twentieth century. Its last resident was Lewis Kilborn, who lived his entire life on the island until his death in 1984.

Local histories record that fishermen and farmers settled on Grape Island throughout the eighteenth century, and like Plum Island, Grape Island had a somewhat sizeable population by the 1870s. By the late 1800s there was a hotel, operated by the MacKinney family, a school where Grape Island's children attended class from April to November, and a number of small cottages and houses owned by seasonal and year-round residents. Summer on the island saw additional residents, and the island and its surroundings was popular with duck hunters, fishermen, lobstermen, and clammers.

The island witnessed considerable decline beginning in the 1920s as more and more families left for the towns of Ipswich, Rowley, Newbury, Newburyport, and other towns. By the 1930s, only the Kilborn family and one other remained. Soon thereafter the Department of the Interior took possession of the island, and it became part of the Parker River Wildlife Refuge. John Kilborn and his son Lewis refused to leave, however, and paid the government monthly rent of $10.00 a month to stay on the island. John Kilborn died in 1946, and for the next thirty-eight years the only residents on Grape Island were Lewis Kilborn and the island's wildlife.

Lewis Kilborn was well known in the area, and hated being sometimes referred to as the "Hermit of Grape Island." He continued to live there much like earlier generations had, collecting rain water for his water supply, heating his home with a wood stove, fishing, and going into town in his boat for groceries. He listened to the world's events through a transistor radio, and would read books and newspapers that friends and relatives would bring him.

I first heard about Lew Kilborn in the early sixties, when my cousin Kilton Brown of Rowley showed me a newspaper story about him. I remember that Lew ran out of firewood one winter and was so cold he said, "I like to have died."

Lew Kilborn died in March of 1984.

I once worked with another welder at Industrial Cab Company of Essex, Massachusetts, from 1964 to 1972, whose name was Abel Beaulieu of Ipswich. One day during that era, Abe took me down the Ipswich River in his 16-foot lap strake power boat and over to the mud flats between Grape and Plum Islands. We dug clams there for a while in that quiet area without realizing that Lew Kilborn was somewhere behind the trees and bushes that had grown up there like a jungle. We heard nothing but a few seagulls.

In about an hour we moved over to the big sandbar to the west of Grape Island to look for clams in that area. Abe had a couple of swim suits in the boat, so I put one on and went for a swim. The bottom there was hard-packed smooth sand, tapering down sharply, so you only had to walk a few steps and you were in deep water. The water was almost warm, and I had a real enjoyable swim for about a half an hour. Then we packed up and returned upriver to the launching area above Melanson's boat shop, and called it a day.

Little remains of the homes, cottages, school, and the hotel on Grape Island. What wasn't torn down or removed by the government was long ago reclaimed by nature.

THE COPPER SPIKE

In the late fifties, I worked for a plumber, Orren Chadwick, at Manchester, Massachusetts. Now and then, we repaired plumbing at the ocean side Weems estate in east Manchester. This property was adjacent to Kettle Island, a small rock about a hundred yards off the beach there.

While working at the Weems estate around 1960, their caretaker, Alexander MacDonald, showed us two bushel-baskets of copper spikes and other metal objects recovered from the site where the wooden battleship *New Hampshire* sunk at Kettle Island in 1922. A rotted ship's timber about five feet long, that had a few copper spikes sticking out of it, was leaning against the garage wall. Mr. MacDonald said the metal in the baskets would be sold for scrap, and the old timber would be saved.

Mr. MacDonald gave me one of the spikes, which is 15-1/2 inches long, seven-eighths of an inch in diameter, weighs two pounds and 14 ounces, and has a 55-degree bend in the middle. The bend may have occurred when the ship struck the rocks, or after it had rotted and settled down through the years.

A friend of mine has a well-illustrated book about shipwrecks, which shows the *New Hampshire* resting in the mud in a very dilapidated condition in the Hudson River before it was raised and towed toward the Bay of Fundy to be scrapped. While being towed, the ship broke away in a storm, and sank at Kettle Island. The book I have referred to says the ship sunk, "...off Graves Island, near Cape Ann," and information found on the Internet claims it sunk "...near Halfway Rock," but I know the wreck site was Kettle Island. I have seen a salvage ship working there. The illustrated book also says, "New England scuba divers have brought up from the vessel many copper spikes said to have been wrought in Paul Revere's foundry."

The *New Hampshire* was built at Portsmouth Navy Yard during the period from 1819 to 1825.

R. LaForest Perkins holding the antique copper spike salvaged from the New Hampshire wreck site. Courtesy Old Mill Mall, Waldoboro

ELMER BOYD, MARINE MECHANIC

I had heard tales of Elmer Boyd, a master marine mechanic, and had heard what a comical guy he was, probably back in the forties.

In 1962, I had an opportunity to work with him. At that time, he was a good-natured, tall, lanky, gray haired, pipe smoking widowed man who was around eighty years old. I had taken a temporary job then, working for George D. Grant Company, automotive and marine carburetion and ignition specialists at Salem, Massachusetts, and met Elmer there. We would both be sent out individually or paired up to work on boats in Marblehead and other close-by harbors.

As we worked together, Elmer told me a lot of interesting stories about his life and occupation. As a young fellow living around Boston, he was walking across a bridge one day and spotted many ships and small boats tied up in a harbor there. He stopped and looked around for a while, and became fascinated with boats, deciding then he wanted to earn his living working on them.

Elmer owned about a forty-foot work boat, a floating machine shop, named the *Queen Mary*, which he moored in Marblehead harbor. It was equipped with a 110- volt electric generator, which provided the power to run his machinery, including a full-size metal turning lathe.

Elmer was once asked to take a marine engine apart that was notorious for burning out connecting rod bearings, and look for a cause. He decided the oiling system was flawed, and drilled an oil access hole in the side of each rod so they would be better lubricated, curing the problem.

Once, Elmer boarded a boat to diagnose a problem and make the necessary repairs. He decided to start the engine first, which caused a gasoline fume explosion that blew him out of the boat and into Marblehead Harbor. He wasn't seriously burned and soon recovered. He suspected someone else had tried to repair the fuel system, and must have left a fuel line dripping.

During one of the hurricanes that hit the Massachusetts coast in the forties or fifties, Elmer decided he would stay aboard the *Queen Mary*, and ride out the storm at anchor in the harbor. He stayed up all night,

A Taste for Salt Water

with his engine running at a little more than an idle to take some of the strain off his mooring lines.

He said his biggest fear during the storm was the possibility of a yacht parting its mooring line and bearing down on him. Luckily, that didn't happen. Elmer said he wasn't anxious to try that again.

Elmer and I were sent out to work on a nice boat, about thirty five feet long, on a breezy day. We usually rode the Boston Yacht Club's launch to get to our jobs, but that day we used a twelve-foot tender with Elmer's outboard motor on it. The motor was an older model with no gear shift, and it had a balky carburetor. As we neared our job, the stiff breeze whipped up a chop. The bouncing tender and yacht were both yawing from side to side, and I could not pull alongside well. Things got out of control, and we hit the mahogany transom, leaving a dent in it about the size of a quarter. Elmer had been sitting in the bow seat, looking aft, and he was thrown toward the bow and down to the bottom of the boat, leaving his legs sticking up in the air. It looked so funny, I could not help laughing. Luckily, Elmer was not hurt, but it was no laughing matter.

Elmer brought his hand tools to the job in a leather satchel. He often brought a thermos of black coffee with him. Wanting a drink, he would pull an old brown-stained tuna fish can out of the bag that he used to wash oily parts in solvent, put a little coffee in it, and swish it around to "clean" it. After throwing that out, he would fill it near full with more coffee, and drink it. When I said he ought not to drink out of that can, he said, "What the hell's the difference?" I tried to tell him what I thought the difference was, but he was not impressed.

One day, after working on a boat in the harbor, I stepped off into the launch, and noticed a cloud of smoke coming out of a forecastle hatch on an expensive two-masted sailing vessel. The ship appeared to be on fire, so we sped over and I jumped aboard it armed with the launch's fire extinguisher. Flames were visible below, and the toxic smoke was thickening, but I managed to discharge the whole contents of the extinguisher down the hatch. Other yachtsmen were arriving, and were fighting the fire from an aft position.

A young man of about twenty years old appeared on deck with burned hands, looking dejected. We helped him into the launch and took him to shore, where an ambulance was waiting for him. The local newspaper said the young man was a student from Germany who was hired by the yacht's owner to remove cabin paint with flammable remover. He had tried to light an alcohol stove to make coffee and the solvent fumes exploded, setting the yacht afire. The fire was extinguished, and the boat was saved, but it was considerably damaged.

One day, a motor yacht was about to set out on a cruise, but the engine wouldn't start. Elmer removed a spark plug, and found traces of water in that cylinder, which might have come from an exhaust pipe backup.

Elmer removed all of the spark plugs, and told the owner to heat them on the stove until they were good and hot. He then poured dry gas into each cylinder and cranked the engine over several times while holding his thumbs over the spark plug holes. When the compression strokes built up maximum pressure, it blew past his thumbs, carrying the water and dry gas mix off with it. The hot plugs were replaced, and the engine promptly started, and the yachtsman left on his trip.

Probably the last time I saw Elmer Boyd, he was boarding with a Mrs. Stevens in a residential area of Marblehead.

This is to certify that

RAYMOND L. PERKINS, JR.

HAS SUCCESSFULLY COMPLETED AN EXAMINATION IN THE

USPS BOATING COURSE

GIVEN BY

WAWENOCK **POWER SQUADRON**

A UNIT OF THE UNITED STATES POWER SQUADRONS

12-19-79
DATE

SQUADRON COMMANDER

This is not a Membership Certificate

THE YACHT *EARLY TIMES*

In 1963 I got a job in a washer factory in Everett, Mass. My cousin, Kilton Brown, worked there, and asked me to help him modernize the heating system.

The general manager, Dick Greenleaf, owned about a 38' tuna fishing boat named *Early Times*. It was designed by naval architect, E. Ray Hunt. It had a vee bottom, and was constructed of marine plywood. It had a large V-8 engine, and had a fish spotting tower on it. It was quite fast, reaching speeds of about 35 knots. Smashing through waves at that speed, crackling noises were heard. Uneasy about that, I asked Kilton what he thought about it, and he said the boat was designed to do that.

I was out off Newburyport one day with Dick and his family and relatives. We had a picnic lunch, and Dick caught a giant tuna which he landed in about a half hour.

I was out with them one day in the same area on an afternoon. I was up in the tower, looking for schools of tuna. The sun was out brightly, and the water looked a little yellowish, as though we might have been in shallow water. All of a sudden, I noticed a wide black formation, and thinking we might be running into a reef, I yelled to the helmsman to put the boat in reverse, but neither he nor anyone else made a move, but they were more familiar with those waters than I was. I began to see that the black shape was moving as we neared it. It turned out to be a massive school of mackerel, which broke up into two groups as we sailed into it. We did not catch any, because we were rigged for giant tuna.

In late summer that year, Dick heard a lot of giant tuna were being caught off Provincetown, so he hired a man to take the *Early Times* down there, and he would drive there the next day to go fishing. I was the only other one who got to go when it left Newburyport. We took turns steering, which I found was a lot of work because the boat had a small rudder, and did not respond well.

We went through the Annisquam River, and tied up at a Gloucester Harbor restaurant float, where we ate supper and spent the night.

At dawn, we left for Provincetown. It was a hot, bright sunny day, with a slight haze off in the distance. It probably took us about three

A Taste for Salt Water

hours to get there, only passing a few small boats, and a couple of draggers.

Nearing Provincetown, we came across a buoy with a different number on it than we were looking for. Checking our chart, we changed course, and soon tied up at one of Provincetown's public floats.

After lunch, we went for a cruise in the bay. The water was calm, and we spotted several schools of giant tuna.

Dick arrived in the afternoon, and using another boat's radio, called us in. He came aboard, with a couple more fishing enthusiasts he had brought with him.

We came right back out, and soon, spotting a school of tuna, we headed for it. It divided, and swam by us, turning their sides up so we could spot their large silverly bodies. They came back together after they passed, and we quickly hooked one. Dick worked up quite a sweat, as the huge fish fought for half an hour. We finally hauled it aboard, and sold it back at the wharf. Then we tied up for the night.

After dark, it began to rain heavily, so we dropped the side curtains, which flapped a lot in the wind. We talked about fishing the next day, until we turned in.

After breakfast the next morning, three boats headed out to go fishing in close formation, one behind the other. The *Early Times* was the third boat in the line. The lead boat was owned and operated by Charlie Blouin, a fishing enthusiast often seen in the Massachusetts Bay area. The second boat, which mounted a spearing pulpit, followed close behind Blouin's boat, just off the starboard quarter.

We were only about five minutes out, when a strange thing happened. A tall man dressed only in swim trunks was standing on deck with his back close to Blouin's pilot house, when the following boat began to drift toward it. The man on deck was looking directly at the pulpit approaching, but showed no attempt to dodge it as the two boats came together. The pulpit struck him in the chest, pinning the seemingly startled man against the pilot house for an instant. Then, the colliding boat gradually drifted to starboard, leaving the struck man standing there motionless.

Most of our astonished group were watching the whole thing take place from behind the *Early Times*' windshield. A Mr. Copp, another boat owner who was traveling with us said, "That guy's hurting, that's for sure."

Both of the lead boats kept going, as though nothing had happened.

I have often wondered how this collision was allowed to happen. There was no logical excuse for it. Or why the man who was struck did not even try to run forward or aft. He could have. I don't know if an accident report was ever filed.

After fishing for a few hours that day without catching anything, Dick drove us home, leaving the *Early Times* tied up at Provincetown so he could fish that area again in a few days.

I wondered how the *Early Times* got its name. I may have gotten a hint, when I saw someone aboard pouring a drink from a bottle of Early Times whiskey.

THE AUTHOR

R. Laforest Perkins lived his early life on the North Shores of Massachusetts. In his later years he moved to Waldoboro, Maine. He retired in 2000 after working at Central Lincoln County YMCA for twenty-one years as a Building and Grounds Maintenance Supervisor.

He has worked at various blue collar occupations including plumbing and heating, home building, metal fabrication and store management. He drove school buses in the Damariscotta area for fifteen years. He is a certified weldor and has passed the U.S. Power Squadron boating course.

In the 1980s he began work on establishing the Mid-Coast Maine Promotion for Clean Indoor Air, a non-smokers rights, and anti-smoking education program. He is a member of the Waldoboro Community Garden Club, the Waldoboro Historical Society, and Friends of the Library. Mr. Perkins is also a member of the Friendship Sloop Society.

Copies of "A Taste For Salt Water"
can be purchased from the author at
Perkins Enterprises, 1315 Manktown Road,
Waldoboro, Maine 04572
for $13.95 plus 5½% Maine sales tax - total: $14.70.